TANNADICE IDOLS

Also by Paul Smith

Pittodrie Idols

Shearer Wonderland: Duncan Shearer – the Autobiography

TANNADICE IDOLS

IDOLS

The Story of Dundee United's Cult Heroes

PAUL SMITH

BLACK & WHITE PUBLISHING

First published 2010
by Black & White Publishing Ltd
29 Ocean Drive, Edinburgh EH6 6JL

1 3 5 7 9 10 8 6 4 2   10 11 12 13

ISBN: 978 1 84502 317 1

A CIP catalogue record for this book is available from the British Library.

Typeset by Graham Hales Design, Typesetting, Reproduction
www.grahamhales.co.uk
Printed and bound by MPG Books Ltd, Bodmin

CONTENTS

To Coral, Finlay and Mia – my idols

ACKNOWLEDGEMENTS

WHILE MY name appears on the cover of this book, many others have made valuable contributions along what proved to be an entertaining and educating journey. At Black & White Publishing Campbell Brown, Alison McBride, John Richardson, Janne Moller and the rest of the dedicated team have once again been a pleasure to work with while Mike Murphy's attention to detail in the editing stages was appreciated along with Bill McLoughlin's efforts in sourcing the pictures that tell the story as well as words ever could. Colin MacLeod again did his bit to bring one particular piece of the jigsaw into place. Thanks also to colleague and Dundee United devotee David Dalziel and his friends for volunteering their own heroes while a long line of other Arabs offered welcome promptings. My thanks also go to Hamish McAlpine, Paul Sturrock, Dave Bowman and Craig Brewster for lending their time and warm memories for the purposes of the book as well as Tom Kilcolm, Lawrie Spence, Stephen Simpson and John Paterson for their insightful contributions. Former United captain, director and chairman Doug Smith is also among those who gave the benefit of his considerable experience – he held all of those positions with distinction, but it is through his place as this particular author's uncle that my own interest in Dundee United can be traced back. His achievements in the club's colours have always been a source of immense pride for the whole Smith clan. On that family note, once again my heartfelt love and thanks go to my wife Coral for her support and to Finlay and Mia for making me the proudest dad in the world as well as to both sets of grandparents – mum and dad and Jim and Moira Wright – for their support and encouragement in all we do. As always, it takes a real team effort to get the ball over the line.

FOREWORD BY HAMISH McALPINE

I CONSIDER myself to be a very fortunate man. I lived every little boy's dream as a professional footballer, won trophies and savoured some incredible experiences – but the best part was that I did it with a team I loved. I feel privileged to have been part of Dundee United Football Club.

What is it that makes United so special? Players and managers down through the years have played their part. The bricks and mortar of Tannadice Park are part of the package. More than anything though, the supporters who have stood by generation after generation of teams through thick and thin are the ones who have made 'our' club what it is.

Tannadice Idols is a book as much about those fans as it is about the players they have cheered on. It is very difficult to put into words the thrill a player gets from running out in front of thousands of fervent Arabs at a packed Tannadice. The hairs on the back of your neck stand up, your heart starts beating that bit quicker and you stand that little bit taller.

Players can be described in many ways – as heroes, idols, legends even. What I never lost sight of was the fact that it was the fans who had the most important role to play in all of that. Without them, there would be no heroes.

After all, the supporters are also the ones paying the wages and they deserve to get something back. I like to think I gave good value for money and Dundee United as a football club has been blessed with many, many, many great servants who never failed to give their all when they stepped out onto the park. I worked alongside some wonderful characters at Tannadice, some of whom are profiled in the pages of *Tannadice Idols*. Players in the mould of Ralph Milne could light up any stadium while the likes of Paul Sturrock and David Narey will forever be remembered for their wonderful contributions to the cause. Of course it would take more than one book to cover the careers of all of the loyal and talented men who have worn the club colours with distinction over the years.

Some of the figures in the pages that follow were at the club a matter of months, while some spent a great number of years. What they all share is the fact that they experienced the same thing as I did when they walked out in front of the home crowd and felt the full force of that fanatical backing.

Maybe I'm biased, in fact I know I am, but I've always felt the United supporters are like no others. Old Firm supporters are spoilt because of the success they have had and can get blasé about it. They expect to win trophies every year and they get greedy. Our supporters, on the other hand, have grown used to making the most of every success because they don't know when the next one will appear on the horizon.

Just look at the atmosphere at Hampden in 2010 when Peter Houston's team won the Scottish Cup and at the joy on the faces of the tens of thousands of Arabs who joined in the celebrations at the Final and back in Dundee in the aftermath. It was pure unbridled happiness, the type that I used to see during the good old days when we were doing so well. When we won the League Cup in 1979, the club's first ever trophy, the emotion of the occasion brought grown men to tears – players and supporters alike.

The type of passion the fans have for the team is exactly the same fervour they have for individual players and once you have them on your side it's a very powerful thing indeed. I really enjoyed my relationship with the supporters and if you had asked any one of the other 19 men featured in this book I'm sure they would have said the same thing.

The surroundings have changed mind you. Back when Duncan Hutchison and his peers were plying their trade it was a very different Tannadice Park to the one that David Goodwillie and Jon Daly perform at today. Even during my time the changes to the fabric of the club were enormous.

Through the 1960s, 70s and 80s I saw the old ground change beyond all recognition as the terraces were built up, the stands took shape and the move towards all-seated stadiums gathered pace. What the development of Tannadice did do was close in the previously wide open spaces and help crank up the atmosphere, making it an even better place to play the game.

Naturally enough I loved playing in front of The Shed in all its glory, it really was a football phenomenon. Time moved on, but the same spirit remains alive and kicking. There's still the same demand for new heroes, new Tannadice Idols, to be born.

INTRODUCTION

FOOTBALL IS a game of rules and structure. Results are recorded, points are won, championships are celebrated and relegations mourned. Oddly though, it is not the certainties in our national obsession that provoke the greatest debate or stir the passions of the hundreds of thousands of football supporters who pour through the turnstiles each season. No, it is the grey areas that have the power to bring down the red mist and pull out the colourful language.

The dubious offside decision, the goal that never was or the contro-versial red card are all bar-room fodder for the beautiful game's unofficial debating societies up and down the land. So too is one of football's other great questions: What is the secret to becoming a hero?

The route to cult status is not an exact science, to which the list of heroes peppered through the history of Dundee United Football Club bears testament. Some have been big, some have been small. Some have been tough, some have been subtle. Some have been long-lasting, some have faded as quickly as they shot to stardom. Some have been enchanting, some have been infuriating. What each and every one has shared, the only common denominator, has been the ability to win the adulation of the people who matter most in the greatest game of all: the fans.

If there was a manual on how to win over a crowd then surely it would be the most read book among football professionals. Unfortunately, the extra special bond between supporter and player is impossible to engineer. It's an organic process that has been part and parcel of the game from day one. Since the first turnstile clicked to let the first paying customer through the door, certain players have had the ability to thrill, to excite and to stoke the passions of the foot soldiers on the terraces and in the stands.

It is the players with that peculiar pulling power who have drawn spectators to our grounds in the hope of seeing something special. Even in the absence of heroes, the hope of seeing a new idol born has always been the optimistic spur to pull on the scarf and brave wind, hail, rain and snow to stay loyal to the cause.

Legends, with their sterling service and admirable consistency, are easy to categorise but the heroes remain something of a mystery. Why is it that certain players have the ability to capture the imagination of a group of supporters and become idols to the masses in what at times has seemed like an instant? The answer, to quote Jimmy Greaves, is that football is indeed a 'funny old game'.

Dundee United is a club that has been blessed with legends and heroes in equal measure. Every generation has had its crop of dedicated and decorated stars who will forever be part of the fabric of Tannadice thanks to their incredible dedication to the cause and the honours they achieved. From as far back as Willie Linn in the 1920s to Doug Smith in the 1960s and '70s, Paul Hegarty in the 1970s and '80s and Maurice Malpas in the 1980s and '90s, there have been wonderful stories of devotion that have elevated a select band to a status way above that of the mere mortals. It takes talent, dedication, imperious presence and the perfect attitude to become a legend.

Tannadice Idols is the second in a series of books delving into Scottish football's love affair with the great characters that have graced the country's many clubs. The starting point has been the definition of 'cult'. It reads: devoted attachment to a person, idea or activity. That, in a nutshell, is the key reference, and the devotion from the Dundee United supporters towards the objects of their affection is at the heart of the matter.

The life and times of twenty individuals who captured the imagination are chronicled. It could just as easily have been forty, fifty or even a hundred who made the final cut since the beauty of the cult hero is that it does not take a consensus of thousands to elevate an individual to those heady heights. An enthusiastic minority of aficionados counts just as strongly in the unpredictable world of football fanaticism.

Some of the names may delight and others may bring furrowed brows and howls of derision. Each, however, has surely staked a claim as a hero in his own way and for his own moment in time.

It is far from a definitive list but is one that has been born from the endorsements of Dundee United supporters of all vintages, with suggestions flowing thick and fast as this particular project gathered pace and more and more people added their opinions to the mix.

Not surprisingly there were names that cropped up time and time again. From Finn Dossing and Hamish McAlpine through to current captain and cult figure Jon Daly, the common threads quickly emerged. Through the process many others began to be woven into the story, with the curious tale of Duncan Hutchison and the enchanting story of Neil Paterson springing up along the way. The crowd-pleasing style of Walter Carlyle, the eccentricities of Ivan Golac and, bringing the story right up to date, the heart-warming cup final heroics of David Goodwillie all merited inclusion in the rich tapestry of Tannadice life.

There are many more in between who have attracted the devoted following of Arabs – whether among tens, hundreds or thousands. Some of the twenty characters studied here, such as Paul Sturrock and David Narey, cross the boundaries between legends and idols. Others, the likes of Jerren Nixon for example, could not touch the all-time greats in terms or achievement or loyalty but still had the X-factor required to make a connection. The beauty of the game we all hold so dear is that there is no formula or even any great logic when it comes to the figures who burn themselves into the memory of the average fan. It is as unpredictable as so many of the stars who have made a lasting impression have been.

There have been goalscorers, rugged defenders, midfield enforcers, tantalising wingers, brilliant goalkeepers and just about every other type of football player you care to mention who have thrilled the masses over the years and right now a new crop is emerging.

When Arabs from all corners of the country descended on Hampden Park in 2010 for the Scottish Cup final there was no telling who would emerge as a new hero. Just as nobody could have predicted the way in which Craig Brewster's life changed on that famous day in 1994 when he became a hero, it was impossible to second guess which stars would rise to the occasion and grab their own slice of history.

Goodwillie and Craig Conway were the headline-grabbing double act but they shared the stage with Jon Daly, a cult hero in the purest sense thanks to the way he has risen from the despair of his injury-riddled early days on Tayside to the responsibility of the club captaincy and the worship of the supporters.

Daly's relationship with the fans has become the stuff of legend and illustrates perfectly all that is good about the bond between the paying public and the paid performers. He has a connection with his devotees that the millionaires of England's Premier League could only dream of, the type of relationship that money simply cannot buy. Just as the heroes of the 1920s and other bygone eras enjoyed camaraderie with the Tannadice faithful, the current generation of players can share that sense of togetherness.

Dundee United Football Club has changed beyond all recognition since the first ball was kicked in 1909 and the city itself bears little resemblance to the one that gave birth to the team at the start of the twentieth century. Yet, through all the changes and the constant evolution, the passion of the supporters has remained as one of the few constants.

There is a perception that hero worship heaped on the modern stars is a relatively new phenomenon. Dig a little deeper and you soon discover that really very little has changed when it comes to the way in which football crowds respond to their idols. The methods may have become more sophisticated with the advent of the internet and mushrooming of television coverage, but supporters of every vintage have always had the privilege of being able to vote with their feet and with their voices. Whether it was the flat-cap brigade of the early twentieth century or the technologically savvy generation which has followed in their brogue-steps, the motivation remains the same and the passions are shared.

Tannadice Idols is about celebrating the past and remembering the entertainers of years gone by, as well as looking to the future and recognising that tomorrow, the next day or the day after that could bring a new hero to be adored. That, after all, is why we keep coming back for more.

1927-1929 and 1935-1939
DUNCAN HUTCHISON

Magic Moment: Hutchison crashed home United's second in a 4-3 win against East Fife to make it thirty-eight goals in the thirty-eight game championship-winning campaign of 1928/29. He lived every striker's dream with the perfect season.

Tangerines Career: Games 215. Goals 122.

THE STORY of Dundee United's idols begins with a man who proved he had the powerful ability to keep the faithful followers away from their beloved club. Duncan 'Hurricane' Hutchison was perhaps the first United man to show just how passionate the club's loyal band of supporters are and always have been. Even in the 1920s, love was most certainly in the air as the influential Fifer brought adoration and infatuation with his daring displays of goal-scoring prowess in the white and black of his adopted team.

> "There may be times when we are powerless to prevent injustice, but there must never be a time when we fail to protest."
>
> **Elie Wiesel, Nobel Prize winner**

Sometimes you don't quite realise what you've got until it's gone and it took the departure of the man they called Hurricane to ram home that message. When Newcastle United lodged a £4,000 bid for the livewire forward in the summer of 1929 it was the type of money that was way beyond the wildest dreams of the Tannadice board.

It was too good to turn down and Hutchison was on his way in a whirlwind.

It was then that Hutchison's status as a hero became clear. In an era where the manager wore a bowler hat and fans attended games in their finest, protests were unheard of. Football was a gentleman's pursuit and a civilised pastime. What the board could not have predicted was the strength of feeling that the departure of the darling of the terraces would provoke, nor the consequences of what, as far as they were concerned, was a sensible piece of business. The money raked in was a welcome boost to the coffers but, as remains the case in the modern game, the devoted fans were more concerned with the team's scoresheet than the club's balance sheet.

Hot on the heels of the threat of a summer drought that led to Dundee being braced to export water to the worst hit areas, temperatures were rising among the disenchanted United supporters.

A hastily arranged boycott was called as supporters plotted to vote with their feet. The plan worked, with a crowd of just over 14,200 assembling at Dens, minus large swathes of the black and white contingent. When the two sides had last played 'over the road' in the league it was during the 1926/27 campaign and more than 20,000 had filed into the ground. With 6,000 fewer turning out in the wake of the Hurricane's sale it was evident the ire was not likely to die down quickly.

Indeed, it is reported that more than 300 made the long and arduous trip by rail and 1920s roads to Tyneside to watch their star man pull on the Newcastle shirt on his debut against Manchester United. He wore familiar shades of black and white, but it was a different crest on his chest and that must have hurt. Still, the Tayside contingent wished their distant hero well in his new life and even presented him with lucky horseshoes as a symbol of their goodwill while they were south of Hadrian's Wall.

It is the boycott of 1929 that demonstrates just how little really has changed when you scratch beneath the surface in our game. Fast forward eighty years to 2009 and the headlines screamed out 'Tannadice Boycott'. Scottish football was in uproar, Rangers supporters were outraged and the end result was a protest of the sort the modern game in this country had never seen. The issue at stake was Dundee United's decision to charge £12 for the visiting support to watch their title-chasing team in action in a match rearranged after the original fixture at Tannadice was rained off at half time. A bitter war of words erupted between the two clubs, with United sticking to their guns and holding their position despite the threat of a revenue draining stay-away policy from the Light Blues support.

Diehard Rangers fans refused to boycott the game but a hardcore did abide by the campaign, orchestrated by the Ibrox club's supporters' trust, and the end result was a crowd just a shade over 10,000. That number was swelled by Arabs determined to prove a point to the opposition and display their loyalty. The figure represented a 2,000 drop on the figure for the corresponding fixture at Tannadice later in the season and highlighted the fact fans still have the power to vote with their feet.

Manchester United fans have recognised that in a far more sustained and precise boycott which has been a cause of considerable concern for the club's owners. Those protesting against the Glazer family's control of their team warmed up for the 2010/11 season by lobbying for a boycott of season tickets by all of those unhappy at the US family's involvement. It was a deliberate attempt to crank up the financial pressure on the success of generating publicity for their green-and-gold cause, with supporters sporting the original colours of the club's first incarnation Newton Heath, rather than the red and black, in a silent protest at the way the club has been run by the current owners and the debt burden currently weighing on the Glazers and United.

Rangers supporters were boycotting an opposition side's ground, attempting to harm United but potentially leaving their own team without backing in a crucial league game. Manchester United fans have actively considered boycotting their own stadium, deliberately aiming to dent the balance sheet as a pressure mechanism.

Both brought substantial interest from the media, but neither was a new tactic. Far from it. As the curious case of Hurricane Hutchsion proves, it was of course Dundee United supporters who can lay claim to masterminding one of the earliest and most orchestrated football boycott protests.

The 1920s were, at least, more civilised than the 1990s and Taysiders, generally, can be considered more mild mannered than their Latin-blooded counterparts in Italy. When Roberto Baggio was sold by Fiorentina to fierce rivals Juventus in 1992 there were full-scale riots on the streets of Florence and furious Viola fans vented their frustration in the form of violence. Fifty people were injured as the protests spilled onto the streets and through piazzas, with Baggio forced to publicly defend his position and stating he was 'compelled' to accept the transfer. He later claimed he would always be a Fiorentina man at heart, a sentiment expressed too late to prevent the riots and one that probably would have had little influence even if it had been more prompt. Those ugly scenes put a modern spin on the strength of feeling the sale of a hero can provoke in a group of fans. The response in Dundee when Hutchison was sold was more muted but there was no questioning the strength of feeling that bubbled beneath the surface. The 1920s supporters had a far more intelligent way of making their feelings known and the 'vote with your feet' tactic is one that, as the 2009 action by the Rangers fans proved, has stood the test of time and remains the only legitimate palpable method of making feelings known.

Hutchison's departure and the reaction to it were big news in the summer of 1929. At around the same time, other issues making the headlines included a message boy's misfortune when his bike crashed on Nelson Street and his load of fruit was scattered across the road for a group of youths to seize upon his misfortune and enjoy an unexpected feast. Solicitor John Ross, of Windsor Street, was also not enjoying the greatest run of luck as his car burst into flames on the corner of Albert Street and Princes Street. The damage was estimated at a wallet-busting £10 to £20. Other incidents in the news included a propensity among Dundee pedestrians to stop and gaze at the recently introduced automatic traffic signals, with "groups of interested men and women" reportedly gathering on street corners to watch the spectacle. It was against that backdrop that word of Hutchison's imminent loss began to filter through to those who chose to get their fix of drama at Tannadice rather than in front of the city's traffic lights. Other bizarre happenings that year included a Carnoustie man requiring an operation to retrieve the false teeth he had inadvertently swallowed. It was headline-making news, but not quite in the same league of the Tannadice revolt of 1929.

Clearly it took a special player to provoke the strength of feeling that greeted the news that Hutchison was moving to Newcastle.

The Kelty-born player was United's very own Baggio, having first appeared on the club's radar in 1927, joining from Dunfermline Athletic, and quickly becoming arguably the first real icon for the supporters of a club still gently feeling its way in the game.

Like the football club, the city too was in transition as the 1930s loomed. The once bustling tram system, which boasted 100 cars at its peak, was being slimmed down and rationalised. At the same time the corporation was busy placing orders for a fleet of new thirty-two-seat buses as a shift in emphasis began to materialise. It was a time of rapid change in all aspects of life and football was just one of those burgeoning areas.

Tannadice crowds at the time averaged 5,000 in the Second Division and Hutchison was ready to play to his audience. From the moment he scored on his debut against Bathgate in front of an appreciative home crowd, he became a player who scored with almost monotonous regularity. In his first season he score thirty-two goals in just thirty-nine league and cup matches. Along that merry way he bagged hat-tricks against Arthurlie and Third Lanark as well as doubles in five other matches. With Hutchison wearing the No.9 shirt, suddenly anything looked possible. There was a player in harness who could turn any game in an instant.

His second season, the 1928/29, proved that to be the case as he led his team to the Second Division championship with a quite stunning display of forward play. Hutchison's record of thirty-four goals in thirty-five games was a major part in the title triumph, with runners-up Morton unable to match United's potency. Manager Jimmy Brownlie's men fell just a single strike short of the 100 mark during a year to remember. Indeed, if Bathgate had not resigned from the league during that campaign the talisman's tally would have stood at thirty-eight goals in thirty-seven matches after a hat-trick in one match against the disbanded side and a single goal in the return fixture. Still, the thirty-four he had to settle for was not a shabby return, and another in the Scottish Cup draw against Dundee, leading to a replay which United won to set up an unsuccessful quarter-final against Rangers, was the finishing touch.

It was a time to rejoice as Dundee United reclaimed their place at the top table of Scottish football and the sense of anticipation was heightened by the presence of a goalscorer who would surely transfer his obvious talents to the new, higher level. And that was the way it panned out, with Hurricane Hutch scoring a double against Clyde on the opening day of the First Division season. A crowd of around 14,000 had flocked to Tannadice to join in the carnival and the crowd pleaser's contribution did not disappoint, helping his side to a credible 3-3 draw on their big day. It was a solid block on which to build a future at that level – or so it seemed.

What followed next was a disaster for the United followers. After just two further games, a 5-2 defeat at Hamilton in which he drew a blank and then a 3-1 win at home to Morton in which he took his total for the season to three goals, Hutchison was gone.

Newcastle United succeeded where other English sides had failed and it came just days before the first derby of the season. Hutchison made his entrance at St James' Park against Manchester United while back at Tannadice the proceeds of the sale were being safely tucked away in the now bulging coffers.

The £4,000 fee was hugely significant. Although it was short of the British record, which stood at a touch under £11,000 following the move from Bolton to Arsenal by David Jack in 1928, it was still among the highest-ranking Anglo-Scottish deals brokered during the era. Newcastle United were no shrinking violets when it came to splashing the cash for Scottish talent. In 1925 the black and whites had dug deep to fund the £6,500 it took to recruit Hughie Gallacher from Airdrie. Mind you, they made their money back on Gallacher when he was sold on to Chelsea in 1930 for £10,000. In Gallacher they had also purchased a player who remains Scotland's most potent international goalscorer, with a ratio of 1.15 goals for every game. His haul of twenty-three goals in just twenty appearances in dark blue was a remarkable achievement and it was his form over his eleven-year Scotland career, from 1924 to 1935, that ensured Hutchison was never capped despite his own strong record as a Dundee United player.

Gallacher knew a good forward when he saw one and had a hand in Hutchison's move to England, having recommended him to the north-east side while still on the playing staff himself. He had travelled north to report on United's progress for a newspaper and witnessed a two-goal blast by the man with dynamite in his boots. It was revealed years later that Jimmy Brownlie had urged Gallacher to boost his player's profile, clearly hoping in turn for a boost to the Tannadice coffers as a result. The plan worked, although the supporters so angered by the deal had no idea of the cogs that were spinning beneath the surface to engineer the outcome. It transpired that the United man was a ready-made replacement for the London-bound frontman who had given him such a glowing reference. Even in the 1920s, long before the first football agent had concluded their first deal, the inner workings of the transfer system were a complex and intricately weaved web. Those on the inside knew exactly how it worked and how to play it to their club's advantage while the man on the street was blissfully unaware as he paid his money at the gate.

Regardless of how United contrived to net such a huge fee for their star man, the scale of the deal cannot be overstated. In 1930 an average three-bedroom house in Britain cost £300 – so United's board could quite happily have gone out and bought an entire street with their windfall. They didn't, but the money was very welcome having invested heavily in the Tannadice infrastructure just four years earlier when the pitch was levelled, new drains installed and the first terracing constructed along with turnstiles. In addition to the improvements made to the changing facilities and club rooms at the ground, the cost was considerable. To put the fee in further perspective, the average annual wage in the UK in 1930 was £200. Newcastle were willing to pay twenty times that amount to get their man. They were also willing to pay the equivalent of 200,000 pints of beer at the going rate of two pence per tankard. The United directors understandably would raise a toast to that sort of money, the equivalent of well over £500,000 in today's terms. Just as the current Tannadice custodians would agree every player has his price, the situation in the 1920s was no different at all. With the great depression of the 1930s on the horizon, money was taking on greater and greater significance in every industry.

The sale of the main asset was a sensible course of action for Dundee United to take, but try telling that to the supporters who had boycotted the ground on the back of Hutchison's departure. Without his services Brownlie's team struggled to build upon their encouraging form in the opening matches of the season and soon fell into the relegation mire. They hit rock bottom at the turn of the year, dropping to the foot of the table after a 4-1 reverse at Cowdenbeath. Although United managed to lift themselves off the bottom, consigning St Johnstone to the wooden spoon, the best they could muster was nineteenth spot and relegation had looked a certainty from Christmas on. Hutchison's goals would surely have lifted the team further up the table and preserved their First Division status, but Brownlie and his board had been happy to take the gamble. It did not pay off and instead they were left with a team relegated back down to the Second Division after just one unhappy campaign and with a set of supporters who, although back in numbers after the short boycott, had been deeply upset by the whole Hutchison episode.

It was not a time to be upsetting the applecart or run the risk of pushing supporters away from Tannadice. Although football was carving out a niche as the entertainment of choice for the working man, there was serious competition shaping up in the form of the burgeoning cinema scene. The 1920s saw picture houses becoming common on every main street in every city and town in the country. In Dundee alone there were more than thirty picture houses, now long since disappeared, with the likes of the Capitol on the Seagate and the Regent on Main Street among those that were in their prime while Hutchison was at his goal-scoring best for United. The new kid on the block was the Alhambra on Bellfied Street and Ure Street, which doubled as a theatre as well as a cinema. With the advent of sound to accompany the latest releases, the entertainers on the football pitches of Scotland's senior grounds had to be on their toes to ensure they could draw paying customers in the same way the personalities of the big screen were doing during that golden age. The 'talkies' were proving popular, although Dundee's culture vultures also set a new record for book reading in 1929 when 96,000 titles were borrowed during August of that year. Dancehalls, according to reports, were also doing roaring trade as the entertainment options continued to expand and excite the Tayside public.

Other sporting activities vying for attention in 1929 included the new open speed meetings on Monifieth sands, introduced by the Dundee Western Motor Club and attracting decent galleries of spectators enticed by the lure of high-octane thrills and spills and the novelty value of seeing cars stretched to their limits.

Those who did have their faith in United blunted by Hutchison's departure were not short of alternatives but it was time to forgive and forget when the 1930/31 Second Division season was launched. Life after Hutchison began. Brownlie steered his charges to the runners-up place and automatic promotion, finding two new hot-shots to try and fill the boots of the missing hero. Jacky Kay took on the challenge and responded with twenty-six goals in forty appearances in the league and Scottish Cup while Williamson hit twenty-two in thirty-eight games. Hutchison was not forgotten, but the performances that season at least numbed the pain of his loss. The stay in the First Division again lasted just a single season as the yoyo years continued for United, who by then were under the control of Brownlie's successor Willie Reid.

Hutchison, who died in 1973, returned to Tannadice as a player in 1935 after spells with Derby County and Hull City. He spent four seasons in the squad and later served as a director, joining the board in 1953 and rising to become chairman for a period in the 1960s. Outside of the game he had built up his pub business, establishing the United Bar on Castle Street in the city centre. The premises are better known now as Kennedy's steakhouse, but in Hutchison's business heyday his football pub attracted Arabs in their droves as they voted with their feet in the same way they had done in his illustrious playing days. Once a hero, always a hero.

1936-1937

NEIL PATERSON

Magic Moment: The ballots are cast and the votes are counted, Paterson becomes United's elected captain and the first amateur to skipper a professional side.

Tangerines Career: Games 27. Goals 9.

TO WIN an Academy Award in the shadow of the Hollywood hills and to captain Dundee United. They are two honours separated by the width of the Atlantic Ocean yet a pair of accolades famously achieved by Neil Paterson. The Oscar-winning forward's incredible story represents a fitting next chapter to turn to in the script of the *Tannadice Idols*, that group of men who more than most succeeded in reaching out to the supporters and making them proud to be part of a club that has been home to some of Scottish football's greatest characters.

Paterson is one of a band of stars who stood out from the crowd to be taken to heart by the Tannadice faithful for reasons not entirely football related. He shares that bond with players from across the generations, some idolised for their physical stature and others on the strength of outstanding personalities, but is unique in the way in which his cult status has evolved over time and did not peak until well after he had kicked his last ball.

It was in 2010 on the fiftieth anniversary of his Oscar win, having been awarded the best screenplay for his acclaimed work on *Room At The Top* in 1960, that Paterson's name was brought back to the fore and his association with United to a new audience. Half a century ago it was his brilliance as a wordsmith that prevented *Ben Hur* from being awarded a twelfth Academy Award and established the modest man from Banff as one of the most brilliant writers Scotland has ever produced.

Yet it was his accomplishments with a ball at his feet rather than pen in his hand that gave Paterson as much satisfaction. This Oscar winner was as interested in Tannadice as he was absorbed in Hollywood, classing his appointment as skipper of Dundee United in 1936 as one of the proudest moments in his twin careers in football and the arts.

Paterson's family, quite rightly proud of his Academy Award honour, have often testified to the fact he would have been just as keen to lead United out at Tannadice as he would have been to repeat the world of film's greatest red carpet walk at the Academy. It was an honest admission from a man who earned the captaincy the hard way, having to win over an entire squad during an era in which fellow players voted to choose their leader.

> "The Oscar is the most valuable, but least expensive, item of worldwide public relations ever invented by any industry."
>
> **Frank Capra, film director**

He won that ballot in the 1930s and that result as much as anything points towards Paterson's popularity during his sporting heyday. Just as he won over his fellow players, the stopper also gained the appreciation of the Tannadice crowd with his displays at inside forward.

He had arrived in Dundee from Edinburgh, having graduated from the capital city's university, and decided to embark on a career in newspapers. Where else to head for, other than the town of jute, jam and journalism? Paterson was taken under the wing of DC Thomson as an ambitious and talented young writer but was also able to indulge his sporting passions while on the staff. Having played for Highland League outfit Buckie Thistle and then Leith Athletic, he already had a track record as a more than decent player and soon found a home at Dundee United, a club still in its infancy when he joined as a twenty-one-year-old amateur in 1936.

From the formation of Dundee Hibs in 1909 and the introduction to life in the Second Division to the change in name and direction when Dundee United burst into life in 1923, the formative years were all about establishing a place in the league structure. When the promotion of 1925 was followed by relegation in 1927 and then the promotions of 1929 and 1931 were followed by relegation in each of the following seasons, a long period was spent regrouping on and off the field in the Second Division before the great strides of the post-war years were made.

While there were no prizes in that period, it was not a totally barren experience for the Tannadice supporters. While they could not celebrate silverware success they did have the joy brought by a succession of talented, devoted and entertaining players.

Paterson was among that number, albeit as a one-season wonder. Within a single season on the books he had made his debut, scored his first goal, been appointed captain, bagged his first hat-trick and then departed. It must rank as the single most extravagant campaign ever recorded by a United star, and in itself would not have been out of place on a movie script as the unknown youngster rose to prominence and high office having been singled out by his peers as a born leader. All the story lacked, in football terms at least, was a happy ending.

After twenty-six games and ten goals, the inside left stood down as captain of the team and took a step back from football completely to concentrate on his burgeoning career as a journalist. Although he made a cameo appearance the following season as emergency cover, it was a one-night-only performance. His decision was final and writing became his sole focus from then on.

At least he could reflect on a season full of highs and lows and cherish his place on the illustrious list of Tannadice captains. He had been introduced to charismatic manager Jimmy Brownlie's side at the start of the 1936/37 season, blooded against King's Park in a 4-2 win in Stirling to set the ball rolling on his career in the senior game, as he pulled on the black-and-white hoops for the first time. The only difference between the new recruit and the majority of those he was playing with and against was that he had retained his amateur status, rejecting the lure of a footballer's wage and instead playing for the love of the game.

He had joined a team that had finished seventh in the Second Division the previous term and hopes were high that a promotion push would ensue. Instead United found themselves competing at the other end of the table and, after his successful maiden appearance, Paterson's next eight games yielded not a single win. It was a desperate time for the club on and off the field, with Brownlie eventually edged out on financial grounds as George Greig came in to take control as the new managing director. Greig had provided the finance to keep the club alive during a time of severe hardship but struggled to improve playing fortunes. Brownlie had been something of a playing icon himself, as the goalkeeper for Third Lanark and Scotland, and had been a major personality following his initial appointment to the manager's role in 1923. Brownlie had been the driving force behind the progressive move to full-time football and had presided over exciting times, but with the club tightening its belt in order to stave off the threat to its existence there was no room for the luxury of a high-profile manager. Greig took on the duties of looking after team matters himself, although training was left to more qualified members of the football staff.

Aside from a six-game unbeaten run in an around November 1936, a run which included a hat-trick for emerging star Paterson in a 5-0 demolition of Forfar at Tannadice and a double in a 5-4 win at Dumbarton, it remained a year of constant struggle. United limped over the finish line as the fourteenth of eighteen teams in the second tier of Scottish football and as they did they were preparing to bid farewell to a forward who should have been at the start of his career rather than marking the end of it.

Paterson, who had added a Scottish Cup goal to his CV when he countered against Airdrie in a 3-1 defeat by the Diamonds during his one and only season, could at least take a modicum of comfort in the fact that he had not exited on the crest of a wave for United. It was very much a case of 'as you were' in the wake of the skipper's departure, with the team continuing to dot around the bottom half of the Second Division in the years before the war.

As much as Paterson protested in later years that his one season as skipper meant as much to him as any of his achievements later in life, it is difficult to imagine he did not sit back at his beloved Crieff home and reflect in his dotage on an immensely satisfying life as a journalist, author and writer. He travelled the world, mixed with some of the most famous celebrities in popular culture and won awards at every turn.

He had cut his teeth with DC Thomson as a magazine writer, sports journalist and then sub-editor before life was interrupted by the outbreak of war in 1939, serving in the Navy during that period. When peace was restored there was a change in direction. He moved away from newspapers and turned to writing books and short stories, with his first novel, *The China Run*, crowned book of the year by the *New York Times*.

Another of his books, *Scotch Settlement*, was adapted for the silver screen and became the basis for the renowned film *The Kidnappers*. That gave him a huge break in America and earned him the opportunity to write the screenplay to the John Braine novel *Room At The Top* in 1959. The film was an instant hit and won him the best adapted screenplay award at the following year's glittering Oscars ceremony.

Paterson did not make the trip to Hollywood personally to accept the award but soon took delivery of the distinctive gold prize back on home soil. Indeed, it was used as a doorstop in later years by his son Kerr after he inherited the statuette following his father's death in 1995. Dad would definitely have approved, having been proud but not precious about his trade. His decision not to relocate permanently to California had ensured his feet never left the ground but he did not have to be in the heart of the action to be a key player. When you are an Oscar winner, demand ensures geography is never a barrier to success and that glittering Academy Awards ceremony in 1960 ensured his life had changed forever.

In the end *Ben Hur* won eleven of the twelve awards it was nominated for, only outdone by the plucky Scot's brilliant effort. It made Paterson a man in demand in Hollywood and he was passionate about his work, refusing to bow to studio pressure and remaining principled about the values of every project he worked on. He wanted perfection and would never compromise.

Although he spent large portions of his life working in the USA, Paterson remained rooted in Perthshire and would shuttle back and forth across the Atlantic to meet his commitments in the film industry. He went on to serve on a variety of British and Scottish film bodies as well as working in television prior to his retirement. He served on the boards of Grampian Television, Films of Scotland, the National Film School, the Scottish Arts Council, the Arts Council for Great Britain, the Pitlochry Festival Theatre and the British Film Institute as organisations flocked to take advantage of his experience, expertise and insight.

Paterson, who was keen golfer and angler, died in 1995 at the age of seventy-nine and his Oscar was passed on first to eldest son Kerr and then, upon his death in 2004, to youngest son John.

John, now based in the rolling farmland of Gloucester, told me:

'Because I was born in the 1950s, after my father's football career was over, I never saw him play, so the memories he passed on from that period in his life are those that I have. He had the odd picture and memento from that time, but we don't have any jerseys. I don't believe they got to keep them at that time.

'In terms of how he regarded his playing days, I know it was a highlight in his life. He thoroughly enjoyed his time with Dundee United and the fact he was the only amateur captain of a professional team was something he felt extremely proud of.

'Whether he thought it was more significant than winning his transatlantic award for writing I could not possibly say; both were achievements that he and the whole family are proud of.

'My daughter has the Oscar now. I'm absolutely sure we will always have immense pride that he is one of the few Scots ever to win an Academy Award – but when you consider it happened a long time ago, it isn't something that is a major conversation piece for us. Life moves on I suppose, but we will always be proud.'

John grew up in Perthshire but admits he was not bitten by the football bug in the same way his dad was, with his interest in the game stemming purely from his esteemed father's role in the Tannadice story.

He added: 'He enjoyed himself as a footballer and although he did not have any involvement in the game after he stopped playing, he certainly always maintained an interest and had a very soft spot for Dundee United. We moved to Crieff when I was just five years old, so we grew up not too far from where his football career had been played out in Dundee. I have to say I was no good at football and, having attended rugby-playing schools, there wouldn't have been an opportunity to play even if I had wanted to. My son plays polo and has a very good eye for that – so the sporting gene has been carried on.'

While John is now embedded in an English way of life, his family tree has branches throughout Scotland. Neil Paterson had links to Dundee through his shot at football glory, Perthshire through his love of the area, Edinburgh through his studies, Greenock through birth and Banffshire due to the time spent as a young man growing up in Banff. A true Scottish hero. As the son of a solicitor, he left Banff Academy to study the arts at Edinburgh University, choosing a different and far higher-profile path than his father. His achievements have been remembered in exhibitions since his death but more importantly in the shape of an impressive literary and film legacy.

When Paterson walked out of Tannadice for the final time in 1937 it marked his final formal involvement in senior football as he prepared to embrace a brave new world in the arts.

He had arrived in Dundee as the city, like the rest of Britain, battled to overcome the Great Depression. He was fortunate to have landed in the area to work in journalism, which along with the jam-making factories was still strong. Jute had been hit hard by the economics of the era and other intensive industries throughout Scotland, such as shipbuilding, struggled.

The post-war years of the 1920s had brought hope and optimism, with society bounding forward and Dundee embracing the culture of inclusion with the first wave of council house construction. At the turn of the twentieth century Dundee's population stood at 161,000, ahead of north-east neighbour Aberdeen. Edinburgh, by comparison, numbered a relatively modest 317,000 with the buzzing port community of Leith removed from the equation. Given Dundee's rapid growth during the period, housing problems had risen to the surface and the overcrowding in the tenements was a major concern. The council house building programme of the 1920s and 1930s helped address the situation.

What was more difficult to address was the arrest and decline of the jute industry, a sector which at the turn of the century had employed almost half of the city's population. Competition from India provided a mountain to climb for the Dundee firms, including the big two of Jute Industries and Low and Bonar. Protection for the industry helped keep it alive through the difficulties of the 1930s but the troubles in what had been a staple of Dundee life cast a shadow over life in Tayside.

It was a time of rising unemployment and of grim hardships, which made the release of sport all the more important as an escape from the realities of life. Other less earthy pursuits had disappeared during the period of austerity, with the Dundee

Theatre transformed into a picture house in a cost-cutting measure to deprive the city of a grand stage setting. While the performing arts were a victim, the drama provided at Dens and Tannadice continued unabashed in the face of the testing financial circumstances. The pinch had been felt at United, where managing director George Greig went as far as handing the entire squad free transfers ahead of the summer break in 1938 to ensure the club did not have to pay wages over the close season. Greig had turned loss into profit and departed with his mission achieved, paving the way for Jimmy Brownlie to return as manager.

Dundee had yet to be overtaken by their more youthful city rivals, with the Dark Blues part of the First Division establishment throughout the 1930s as they troubled neither the championship challengers or had to concern themselves with the relegation struggles at the other end of the table. Instead, they had the comfort of mid-table mediocrity. That remained the case until 1938, when the Dens men tumbled from their safe perch in the First Division after finishing second bottom of the top league. Along with Morton they were relegated. It brought a brief return for the league derby before the war years and also brought a sense of parity to football in Dundee as the city's two teams landed at the same level.

The war years that followed hard on the heels of Paterson's captaincy brought their share of crowd pleasers, players able to lift the spirits in a time of dire need. Norwegian guests Boye Karlsen and John Sveinsson thrilled the crowds while Bert Juliussen's run of ninety-four goals in eighty-one wartime games made him an obvious hit. Juliussen, the exotically named Englishman who found himself stationed in Perth with the Black Watch, had been on the books of Huddersfield Town previously but it was with

United that he made his first significant impact. He was a powerful striker and, as the son of a Norwegian, had inherited his father's Scandinavian athleticism. That led to a fierce shot and the confidence to fire in efforts from all angles and from every distance.

His performances during the war obviously caught admiring glances, first turning out for Dundee before returning to his home country to play for Portsmouth after the south-coast club had invested £11,000 in him. Juliussen then became Everton's record signing when he switched to Goodison in 1948 for the similarly hansome fee of £10,500. He scored just a single goal for the Toffees, played just ten games and then disappeared into the lower leagues with Consett in his native north-east. Legend has it that Juliussen's failure to hit the heights with Everton could be attributed to the affliction of varicose veins, a condition which is also reputed to be behind his odd custom of being reluctant to undress in front of team-mates at Pompey. He is said to have taken that peculiarity to extremes, even taking to the communal bath with his football socks still firmly in place.

The suggestion is that Juliussen rejected medical advice to quit the game and his judgement proved right as he battled on with the enthusiasm which had made him a success with both Dundee sides. He returned briefly to the Scottish scene with Berwick Rangers and Brechin City in the 1950s, helping the Angus side to promotion in 1954 to sign off on a high note and bring to an end an eventful career in the senior game.

The Englishman may be remembered as something of a misfit on Merseyside, but on Tayside he remains a record holder. His six-goal haul against St Bernard's in 1941 remains the best return for a player in a single match for the club, albeit outside the confines of competitive action due to the war.

It was characters like Juliussen who created a buzz at Tannadice during the 1930s and '40s, keeping spirits high at a time when events outside of football cast a long dark shadow over life. As peace broke out and the economic situation improved across the land, the next group of entertainers was waiting in the wings primed and ready to bring a ray of sunshine to the bright side of the street.

1960-1963
WALTER CARLYLE

Magic Moment: With the flag fluttering in front of him, the wing wonder's repertoire of impromptu goals during his brief but eventful stay at Tannadice continued to build with a strike straight from a corner.

Tangerines Career: Games 103. Goals 45.

CONSOLIDATION IS the name of the game for every club that wins promotion. Fanciful dreams of free-flowing football and goal bonanzas on the new big stage are filed away for another day as the need for solidity and security comes to the fore. What you need after stepping up a level are battle-hardened professionals with the experience required to fight tooth and nail to cling onto the cherished place the club spent the whole of the previous season working so hard to win.

Unless, of course, you happen to be Jerry Kerr. The lauded and revered Dundee United manager earned his place in Tannadice folklore when he guided his men from the Second Division to the top flight at the first attempt in the 1959/60 season. It was Kerr who set the ball rolling in the transition from respected club to major force in the Scottish game and when the men in black and white took their place in the First Division in the summer of 1960 they did so with a smattering of new faces.

The club had a love-hate relationship with promotion up to that point. The supporters had enjoyed the jubilation several times in the pre-war years but on each occasion it only led to the disappointment and despair of relegation. Those old enough to remember the pain of previous trips into the First Division must have been riddled with fear as the next tangle with the top names loomed. What if the same frailties were exposed again? What if it was another short and bitter-sweet experience? With those questions in mind, they must also have been hoping for a safety first approach from their trusted manager.

Trusted he may have been, but predictable he was not. Kerr ripped up the promotion-winning manager's manual and instead followed his instincts. Rather than going for brute force as he faced up to the not inconsiderable might of the teams in the elite, he opted for craft and guile. Walter Carlyle was technically already on the books when the Second Division title was won, joining Kerr on the incredible journey when he signed in March 1960 in the final weeks of the triumphant campaign, but it was when the curtain was raised on the First Division campaign in August that year that he came into his own.

> "The best subjects are always people, who never fail to amaze me by their unpredictability."
> **Ronnie James Dio, musician**

Carlyle, just twenty-two and without any senior experience after an apprenticeship on the books of Rangers, was promoted to the starting eleven and given the right-wing berth which would become his own. He was athletic and skilful, the identikit right winger in build and appearance. He had skill to match his frame and had the ability to thrill a crowd with his bursts down the flank and penchant for shooting whenever there was the slightest glimmer of opportunity.

For a wide man, the Falkirk-born attacker had an incredible goal to game ratio. In all competitions he made 103 appearances and netted forty-five times to prove just why he became a favourite in black and white among the supporters. He had a nose for goal and an opportunistic streak, with his haul including one strike straight from a corner kick.

He made his debut against Stirling Albion in a 2-1 victory at Annfield in the League Cup as the 1960/61 season burst into life and kept his place in Kerr's side to run out in front of almost 18,000 people crammed into Tannadice for the first First Division fixture against Hibs.

Carlyle eased himself into the fray that term in confident fashion as Kerr's rookies made a convincing debut at the top table, finishing ninth in the eighteen-team league and ensuring top-flight football was no flash in the pan.

When the 1961/62 campaign rolled around, Carlyle was ready to hit top gear. In thirty appearances in league and cups he scored an impressive seventeen goals to finish one ahead of striker Denis Gillespie in the scoring chart, with the deadly double act helping United continue to build for the future as they recorded another respectable finish, in the top ten of the Scottish game. The new kids on the block had proved more than adept at living in exalted company and the supporters were responding enthusiastically. Even after the honeymoon season had passed, during which time the average home gate touched 12,000 fans, the attendance figures remained over 9,000 on average.

Gillespie and Carlyle became a feared duo but also had a healthy rivalry in the scoring stakes, one that the winger held the upper hand in during his time at the club. In the 1962/63 season, the end-of-season tally stood at twenty-two for Carlyle and eighteen to Gillespie, a forty-goal haul that helped United climb to seventh in the league and into the semi-finals of the Scottish

Cup. The flanker had also claimed a slice of Tannadice history as his own, becoming the first man to score under floodlights at the ground when he grabbed the opener against Rangers on 10 November 1962 as the newly installed bulbs brought night-time football to the United fans.

He was part of a generation grateful to be afforded the opportunity to earn a wage from the game. Like so many of his peers, Carlyle could take nothing for granted as a teenager and served his time as an apprentice coach builder while the dream of sporting stardom remained distant.

For the flying winger and his generation there was no prospect of earning enough from the game to retire wealthy, in stark contrast to the leading players of the modern game. Perhaps that financial parity with the supporters enhanced the relationship between subject and spectator, with the players kept in touch with their working roots by the fact that they knew they would return to labour side by side with those who idolised them once their sporting days were behind them. Because of that, the hero worship took on a different form, although it was no less passionate.

Carlyle earned his status the hard way. He had honed his love of football as a hamper boy at Falkirk and was attracting interest from the Bairns talent spotters when a leg fracture nipped his hopes of a big break with his hometown side in the bud. He overcame that injury to win a place on the Rangers staff but it took his switch to United to bring him to the fore.

Together with Gillespie he thrilled the Tannadice crowd in those fledgling days as a top-flight team. It could be argued that it was the rise to the upper echelons of the Scottish game that changed the face of the club and its key men forever. No longer were United players simply sportsmen, they began to become stars of the soap opera that is football at the highest level. Previously United players mixed in modest circles, among the part-timers of East Fife, Dumbarton, Stranraer, East Stirling, Brechin City... the list goes on and on. It was a worthy existence and an earthy one, but when the Terrors leapt into the First Division in 1960 it brought them into more exalted company. The compact and bijou surroundings of grounds such as Stair Park, Glebe Park and Firs Park were swapped for the sprawling expanses of Parkhead, Ibrox, Tynecastle and Easter Road on a regular basis. The United squad, who up to that point had been working away with a quiet determination, were all of a sudden thrust under the spotlight shared by the Old Firm and the other major forces of the era.

With the extra attention came added adulation from a crowd swelled by the joy of promotion and curiosity about the realities of life in the First Division. The eager Tannadice crowd were looking for heroes and in Carlyle and Gillespie they found two men capable of filling the role in those early days.

More than anything, supporters up and down the land were desperate to embrace entertainers as the austerity of the war years faded into the distance and the vibrancy of the swinging sixties loomed large on the horizon. Carlyle's position on the wing gave him licence to thrill and his unpredictable style ensured he quickly became a favourite.

The 1960s were a golden era for Scottish wingers, with every team sticking rigidly to the traditional formation hinged on having a wide man on each flank. The chosen two had freedom to attack at will and that helped foster the unique talents of some of the finest players the country has ever seen, during a period in which club sides were among the best in Europe. It was that environment that ensured size was no barrier to Willie Henderson becoming a legend with Rangers and that earned Jimmy Johnstone his place in Celtic folklore.

The Old Firm duo, along with the blossoming young figure of Willie Johnston in the blue half of Glasgow, became the most recognised flankers ever to grace the Scottish game but that should not disguise the fact that teams throughout the land had their own wing wizards who in their own style were doing as much to excite their home crowd as Henderson and Johnstone were at Ibrox and Parkhead.

There was Alex Edwards at Dunfermline and Jimmy Smith at Aberdeen and others in the same mould. They were tricky, quick and with an inbuilt desire to press forward at every opportunity. Carlyle was cast from the same mould and had the type of loveable approach to the game that supporters could embrace.

He occupied the right-wing berth for a short but memorable time during a period in which Kerr looked for the combination of flankers that would unlock First Division defences up and down the land. It was Bobby Norris who fell out of the team to make way for the new man, while on the other side of the park a succession of left wingers were called upon during Carlyle's time in the team. Gibby Ormond, Neil Mochan and Ian Mitchell all had a season in possession of the No.11 jersey without quite the same success, particularly in terms of contributing to the goals tally, as their colleague on the right had.

Carlyle moved on to Millwall in November 1963, a move that took him from the pinnacle of the Scottish game down to the lower reaches of the English ladder. He joined a Lions side struggling at the wrong end of the Third Division and his efforts were not enough to prevent them from dropping down to the fourth tier at the end of that term, although they did bounce back at the first attempt.

While his protégé tried his luck south of the border, Kerr had to hope for good fortune in his efforts to replace him in the United line-up. It was a tall order and it took until the arrival of Finn Seeman in the second half of the decade to find a natural successor.

By that time Carlyle was already on his way back, returning to Scotland in 1965 to join Motherwell. He also turned out for St Johnstone and Alloa before retiring and concentrating on a career in the licensed trade and then in coach building. He kept his sporting passions alive through his love of golf and was a member at St Andrew's and Caird Park as well as Carmuirs in Falkirk, moving back to his home town with his family in later life. Carlyle passed away in Falkirk on Hogmanay 2007.

Gillespie, another of the players from the first season in the First Division who won hero status, is also no longer with us. He died in 2001. Gillespie was a different player from Carlyle but brought the same response from the United faithful thanks to his energetic and committed style as well as his goal-scoring ability and talents on the ball.

Gillespie, more than fifty years after he played his first match for the club, remains among the all-time leading scorers for Dundee United. His return of 114 goals in 454 matches tells only part of the story, with Gillespie's contribution to the cause measured in more than black and white statistics. The one figure that does more to bear out Gillespie's popularity is not one recording goals but one charting an attendance. In May 1973 a crowd of 12,500 turned out for the Duntocher-born forward's testimonial match against Dundee. When the 1973/74 season kicked off, a crowd of

4,671 turned out for the first home match against St Johnstone. Gillespie 1 Scottish Football League First Division 0.

He was another Jerry Kerr signing, arriving at Tannadice having first played under Kerr at Alloa. He had already been a thorn in the side of the Terrors while playing for the Recreation Park side, scoring a hat-trick for the Wasps in a 7-1 rout of United on Tayside at the tail end of the 1957/58 campaign. By 1959 he had switched sides, recruited by Kerr following the manager's own move from Alloa to Dundee United, which brought a new focus as well as full-time football to Tannadice for the first time.

Gillespie's eighteen goals in thirty-four league appearances were vital in earning promotion for the club from the Second Division in 1959/60 and fittingly he scored the first ever First Division goal, netting during the curtain-raising 3-1 home victory against Hibs as the 1960/61 season opened. He remained a fixture in the side throughout the 1960s, joining Brechin City in 1971 at the ripe old age of thirty-five. The five-figure gate for his testimonial two years later showed a remarkable strength of feeling for the enthusiastic service from the supporters he left behind, a striker gone but far from forgotten after his decade. Indeed, that enthusiasm did not wane until after his fortieth birthday when Gillespie decided to retire from the game after five years with Brechin. As the pace had faded, the one-time goal king of Tannadice had dropped back through the team and served as a sweeper at Glebe Park. His versatility was nothing new for United fans, who had seen their favourite play in defence, midfield and attack during his time on the staff. He was a man who gave the impression he would have played in goal if asked, such was his passion for the club and for football in general.

That dyed in the wool spirit was a feature of life under Kerr, who was also the man responsible for nurturing the abilities of defender Jimmy Briggs and helping him fulfil his potential to become a hall of fame member and true Tannadice legend.

Briggs had first appeared in the black and white hoops of his hometown team in 1955 when manager Reggie Smith gave him his big break. He deputised in both full back positions during the 1955/56 and 1956/57 campaigns before establishing himself as a regular under manager Tommy Gray the following campaign. National Service ensured the name was missing from the team-sheet for the best part of two years before the stalwart returned to the fold just in time for the promotion celebrations in 1960.

When United took their place in the First Division it was with Briggs very much at the heart of the team, joining Tommy Neilson as the only ever-presents in the league fixtures in 1960/61. The duo also played in all seven cup ties. Briggs played in every fixture during the 1961/62 season too and, not surprisingly, was eventually elevated to the captain's role by an appreciative Jerry Kerr during the 1960s. It was the Dundonian, recruited by the club from St Mary's Youth Club, who led his men out against Barcelona at the Camp Nou when United made their European debut in the Fairs Cup in 1966 and helped them to a 4-1 win on aggregate.

Briggs remained a fixture in the side until two broken legs in the space of twelve months, at either end of 1968, left him sidelined for long periods. He remained on the staff as a back-up player until the summer of 1972, when he joined Montrose to round off a career in which he had been a great servant and a very solid competitor – not to mention a man appreciated by the legions of supporters who followed their team with the same passion with which the man played the game.

Ron Yeats was another crowd pleaser in that respect, with his sheer physical presence and lion heart. The Liverpool legend may have been appointed as an honorary Scouser at a town hall ceremony on Merseyside in 2009, but for the Tannadice masses he will forever be a Terror. After all, it was Dundee United who picked up on the defensive talents of the imposing centre half at a time when it looked as though he would be lost to the senior game forever.

The Aberdonian had been a teenage star at Hilton Academy on the north side of his home town and with the Aberdeen Lads' Club Thistle team that spawned another club hero, Doug Smith. Yeats had won Scotland schoolboy recognition and played junior football with Lads' Club while working as a slaughterman. Trials with Forfar, Falkirk and Bury were unsuccessful but Tommy Gray, then the manager at Tannadice, saw something in the youngster that the other clubs had contrived to miss and he joined the ranks of part-timers at the club. At 6ft 2in tall and powerfully built, his potential should have been obvious but it was Gray who seized upon it and then Jerry Kerr who built on that promise by making him a central figure in the United story.

He would work shifts at an Aberdeen abattoir, sometimes until 3am on the morning of a match, before heading south to indulge his sporting passions. That is the type of commitment and devotion that made the likes of Yeats and Briggs stand out.

By the time promotion was won in 1960, Yeats was the captain and figurehead. He had climbed to the brink of a Scotland call-up by the time Liverpool weighed in with a successful £30,000 offer in the summer of 1961.

It marked the beginning of a love affair between Yeats and his Liverpool public as he went on to captain England's slumbering giants to the Second Division championship, then the FA Cup in 1965 and the First Division championship the following season. He also won two Scotland caps after moving south, remaining on the Anfield staff until moving to Tranmere Rovers in 1971 as a player-coach and then manager. Yeats also had a spell in charge of Barrow before returning to Liverpool as chief scout for a twenty-year assignment, only ended by his retirement in 2006.

The upsurge in the club's fortunes under Kerr had brought a string of big personalities into the spotlight and for the Tannadice faithful it was a time to savour. What they did not know was that their manager had a few more surprises up his sleeve and that Dundee United were ready to bring a cosmopolitan twist to the Scottish game. Exciting times were about to get even more thrilling.

1964-1967
FINN DOSSING

Magic Moment: Dundee are destroyed 5-0 as the Danish star's derby hat-trick completes the Massacre of Dens Park in August 1965 and a hero is born.

Tangerines Career: Games 106. Goals 67.

JERRY KERR'S own playing career took him no further than the highways and byways of Scotland, playing his way up through the ranks from Armadale Rangers through to Rangers, Alloa, St Bernards, and, during the war years, Dundee United before rounding off with Motherwell and Peebles Rovers. As a manager he steered Berwick and Alloa before pitching up at Tannadice to begin his revolution on Tayside in 1959.

He was homegrown and proud, but that background did not prevent him from broadening his horizons as a coach. Kerr proved to be ahead of his time in so many ways and the decision to look to Scandinavia for the talent required to fine tune the United machine he was building proved to be inspired and inspiring in equal measure.

> "It is good to love the unknown."
>
> **Charles Lamb, writer and critic**

The first hint of his grand plan came in the winter of 1964 when he and his Dundee United board began their pursuit of Orjan Persson. The Terrors directors had to be dogged as they attempted to lure the Swedish winger from his club Orgryte, travelling to Gothenburg three times before finally completing the swoop for the highly rated twenty-two-year-old. He had been part of his country's squad for the 1964 European Championships just months earlier and clearly had a big future ahead of him.

Just as the news of Persson's imminent arrival on the Scottish scene was beginning to filter through, after a top-secret signing mission mounted by United, there was another surprise announcement.

This time the new arrival was a Dane by the name of Finn Dossing. Few on Tayside knew much about the powerfully built twenty-three-year-old forward, save for the handful who managed to sneak a glimpse of him during hush-hush bounce games held behind closed doors to allow Kerr to watch his prospective player at close quarters, but the Tannadice faithful would soon find out everything they needed to know about their continental star in the making.

For star-struck Dundonian schoolboy Tom Kilcolm, the great Dane made a lasting impression. Now in his 60s, Kilcolm is a proud founding member of the Finn Dossing Argyll Arabs, a Lochgilphead-based supporters club who have adopted the moniker in homage to the super striker, and has been instrumental in keeping his hero's name alive decades after he crossed the North Sea to return to his homeland.

Kilcolm told me:

'Dundee had won the league in 1962 but at United, for the first time since promotion, there was talk of relegation. It was because of that type of attitude towards United that I chose to support the team – because I loved an underdog.

'I first started going along at the start of the 1960s, when I would have been just twelve. Then all of a sudden Jerry Kerr signed Finn Dossing and everything seemed to change – the transformation was amazing. To me he was like Roy of the Rovers. I was a lad of fifteen and still reading comics like *The Wizard*. Dossing was like he had come straight out of one of those stories with the way he played the game.

'Finn didn't just hit the ball – he blootered it, to use a good old-fashioned word. He didn't try to curl his shots into the top corner or chip the goalkeeper but got his head down and went for power and accuracy. The first thought in his mind when he got the ball was to go for goal and he was just so exciting and wonderful to watch. It was like a messiah had been sent to score goals for us. It didn't matter if we were winning 1-0, losing 2-0 or drawing 1-1 – you always felt as though it was just a matter of time before Dossing got his goal. You knew he would score.'

At 6ft 1in tall and weighing in at 12st 4lb, he had the muscle required to survive at the top level and the nous to exploit his physique to the full. He had been playing as an amateur for Viborg in his homeland, turning out in the Second Division of the Danish pyramid, but was ready to explode at the highest level.

When the European duo arrived they were thrust into a side struggling in the lower reaches of the First Division, sitting sixteenth in the eighteen-side league and in desperate need of a lift. Persson and Dossing were introduced to the side just days after their arrival on Scottish soil at the beginning of December in 1964, named in the starting eleven for a tricky trip to face Hearts in Edinburgh. It ended in defeat for Kerr and his men, with the Jambos running out 3-1 winners, but it was an eventful afternoon for Dossing as he pulled on the No.9 shirt for the first time. He scored a debut goal but had his joy tempered by a booking to mark his introduction to the hurly-burly of the Scottish game, a caution which his new club appealed to have rescinded in the aftermath of the game. The SFA rejected that bid, but it did not dent the new boy's enthusiasm for the task in hand.

One man does not make a team, according to that familiar entry in the book of football adages, but Dossing came very close to doing just that in his maiden campaign. After easing his way into the fold with that goal against Hearts, he hit his stride in fine fashion as the league race entered a crucial phase.

First came a vital goal in a 1-1 draw at Motherwell then another the following week in a 4-1 win at home to St Johnstone. That victory, the first in six matches, proved to be the catalyst for a stunning run of results that hauled United clear of the relegation zone and into the top half of the table.

A first-half double at Tannadice against Celtic after the St Johnstone fixture rocked the Hoops and helped his side to a 3-1 win against the men from Parkhead. The following week, at Easter Road, he went one better – banging in a first-half hat-trick against a beleaguered Hibs to well and truly announce his arrival as one of the Scottish game's most dangerous forwards. Persson added a fourth in the dramatic 4-3 win and it proved to be the third victory in a series of seven that took the club from sixteenth to tenth in the table. In among those games there were five more goals for the unstoppable Dossing, including doubles against St Mirren and Third Lanark.

He scored another brace, in a 6-0 win at home to Clyde, before the season was out and finished the term with twenty-one goals to his credit from nineteen First Division starts as the recovery was completed and the team, lifted by their Danish striker, finished in ninth spot.

By the time the curtain fell on the 1964/65 season there was another Dane on the books at the club, with young attacker

Mogens Berg recruited from top-flight side Odense just a week after Dossing had joined. Berg was just twenty when he upped sticks and headed for the promised land of Scotland, establishing himself immediately as an integral part of Kerr's side.

He and Dossing were among seven Danes plying their trade in the league at that time, with Morton boasting the other five in the shape of Erik Sorensen, Kai Johansen, Carl Bertelsen, Jorn Sorensen and Lief Holten.

Berg's time in Scotland was stalled by a back injury and he underwent surgery in 1965 in an attempt to end his pain. The tall and well-built player lost more than two stone in weight as a result of the operation and bravely attempted to battle back to fighting fitness before eventually giving up on his dream of making it big with Dundee United in 1968.

During the 1964/65 season, Kerr completed his quartet of imports with the experienced Swedish international Lennart Wing. The twenty-nine-year-old, at home playing at left back or left half, had played alongside Persson at Orgryte and had caught the eye of the Terrors during their courtship of his team-mate.

Wing remained with the club for two and a half years, establishing himself as an outstanding performer after taking a leave of absence from his job as a fireman in Gothenburg to sample the professional game in Scotland. When Wing called time on his time at Tannadice in the summer of 1967 he returned to his day job in Sweden after being made to choose between the fire brigade and full-time football by his paymasters back home. With an eye to the future, the thirty-two-year-old opted to return to base. As a measure of the impact Wing made, he was appointed captain for his final game in United colours at Tannadice as he led out the side against Partick Thistle. Later that evening he was crowned the club's player of the year, pipping Dossing to the prize at the annual supporters' function.

By then there was another Scandinavian on the staff, the Norwegian winger Finn Seemann joining in 1965 from Lyn Oslo, and staying for three years before being signed by DWS Amsterdam in the Netherlands in a £25,000 deal in 1968. Seemann died following a car accident in 1985 at the age of forty, but will never be forgotten in Dundee. It was Seemann who scored the decisive goal in United's first-ever European tie, bagging the second in the 2-1 win against Barcelona in Spain in 1966/67 when the side represented Scotland in the Inter-Cities Fairs Cup. A 2-0 win at Tannadice, courtesy of goals from Ian Mitchell and Billy Hainey, completed the job and set up a second-round challenge against the Italian might of Juventus. A 3-0 defeat in Turin put paid to the dreams of further progress in the competition but pride was at least restored when Juve were beaten 1-0 in the return tie on Tayside. Again it was the Scandinavian connection that won the match, with Finn Dossing's stunning overhead kick settling the game in fine fashion in front of a crowd in excess of 27,000.

The refined talents of Dossing, Seemann, Persson and Wing had been key to the win against Juventus but the influx of Scandinavian talent during the 1960s was viewed with suspicion by home players, fearing for their own livelihood as the impressive array of stars carved out glowing reputations. Dundee United's gang of five was replicated with five at Morton, three at Aberdeen and one at Hearts as well as Icelander Thorolf Beck at Rangers. That clutch of players was a concern for the Scottish Players' Union, who discussed the Scandinavian influence as a matter of urgency at a management committee meeting early in 1965 on the back of Wing's arrival on Scottish soil. John Hughes, secretary of the professionals' union at that time, insisted his senior members were more concerned about the prospects for emerging home-grown talent than their own berths in First Division teams – but it was clear feathers were being ruffled by the increasing reliance on faces from overseas to fill their teams.

Given the impact Dossing had following his appearance in the white and black of United, it was an understandable reaction from the union. Dossing's goal-scoring form made him an obvious hero for the fans; his fellow import Persson was making waves in his own way. The cool, composed and cultured left winger oozed class and had the ability to bring serenity to the most tempestuous of games.

As with so many gems unearthed by clubs in the provinces, it did not take long for the cash-rich Old Firm to flex their financial muscle and tempt Persson to the west coast. It was Rangers who set their sights on the Swedish flanker, agreeing to swap star man Davie Wilson and defender Wilson Wood in a bid to secure his services in August 1967. Persson became a regular for the Light Blues under Scot Symon and Davie White before being released to return to Orgryte in 1970, coinciding with his involvement in the 1970 World Cup finals. He went on to win forty-eight caps for Sweden before retiring from the international game in 1974.

The five Europeans never did play in the same United side in a competitive game, although having four in the side at any one time was not uncommon for Kerr during the mid and late 1960s.

Dossing spent three memorable years on Tayside before returning to his home town of Viborg at the end of 1967, leaving with the club's blessing to reclaim his amateur status and con-centrate on building a career outside of football in tandem with his playing commitments back on his old stomping ground that been his springboard to the full-time game during his days with the Danish under-21 squad. After leaving United he went on to run a successful gentleman's outfitters in Denmark, perhaps not a surprising choice given his stylish approach to his sporting profession.

By the time he left Scotland, Dossing's status as a cult hero was assured, not solely because of his very healthy goals to game ratio but more because of one heavenly ninety minutes of football. The date was 11 September 1965 and the venue was Dens Park. The opposition wore dark blue and were well and truly humbled by their rivals from across the road, hammered 5-0 in one of the most memorable derbies ever played out on British football's most famous football street.

The visiting Terrors lined up with Don Mackay in goal, Tommy Millar and Jimmy Briggs at full back and Doug Smith, Lennart Wing and Tommy Neilson at the heart of the side. With Orjan Persson and Benny Rooney wide and Frank Munro and Dennis Gillespie showing their traditional commitment, it was a team with balance and poise. At the tip of that group was Dossing and it was the classy Dane who bagged a famous hat-trick on a glorious afternoon to etch his name into Dundee United folklore. A goal from Gillespie and another by Wing, from the penalty spot, completed the rout and sealed Dundee's embarrassment. Dossing was developing a happy habit of scoring against his side's biggest rivals, having netted during his first taste of the fixture the previous season during a 2-1 win.

What made the 5-0 result all the more remarkable was the fact it came on the back of a 4-0 reverse at home to Celtic on the opening day of the season just a few weeks earlier. Kerr's side did not lack character and the response in the next First Division outing could not have been more resounding. More than 15,000 were packed into Dens to witness the mauling.

Tom Kilcolm was among that number and he recalls:

'The climax to Dossing's career with United was obviously his hat-trick against Dundee at Dens Park. I was there that day and even now, more than forty-five years on, I can remember how it felt when those goals were crashing in. I can still picture Dossing standing there in his white shirt with the black collar, arms outstretched above his head as he celebrated. I can remember it all the better because I had the picture cut out of *The Courier* and stuck on my wall for a good few years after.

'He was there for such a short period of time but his impact was absolutely huge. I can't think of a single player I have seen in a United shirt that has had the same impact. I was playing football myself and I know how much of an influence Dossing's performances had on me. It must have been the same for every schoolboy who spent his Saturday afternoons at Tannadice.

'With Dossing in the side we knew we held the ace in the pack. I would say Dossing was the first real hero, certainly the first that I can remember.

'We were struggling and in real danger of being relegated before he came in and scored the goals that took us well clear of that. He was a big, strong guy with such a fierce shot. He also had ability and you have to wonder where Jerry Kerr first discovered him. However it came about, the signing was a masterstroke. The Scottish game was undoubtedly more physical back then than it is now and he took that in his stride to become the type of player who can change a game in an instant. He was also as strong as an ox. To me, Dossing was a magical figure who had arrived from nowhere.'

Dossing was immortalised, not only in the Massacre of Dens Park song but also in a chant adopted from the *Love Potion No.9* advertising campaign of the era, swapping the original lyric for Finn Dossing No.9 as his popularity soared.

The hat-trick in the Dens demolition got Dossing off the mark for the 1965/66 season and once he started he did not stop. He scored a double in a 5-1 win against St Johnstone in his next outing and was an ever-present in the league that term, scoring an impressive twenty-five times in thirty-four appearances. He haunted Motherwell in particular, scoring hat-tricks in each of the First Division encounters with the Steelmen as he helped United to a fifth-place finish in the top flight.

He was tall, athletic and appeared to glide through games that might normally have seen players bogged down by conditions and the physical battles thrown up by the Scottish game. It ensured his impact far outweighed the time spent on Tayside and the Dossing name remains fondly remembered despite a relatively short association with the club.

From his first game in December 1964 to his last in October 1967 he played 106 games and scored 67 goals. That package comprised eighty-six games in the First Division with a hugely impressive return of sixty goals, eight appearances in the Scottish Cup with five goals, eleven League Cup matches that brought a single goal and his goal against Juventus to give him a 100 per cent strike rate after his one and only European tie for the club.

The Scandinavian experiment ended during the 1967/68 season when Dossing, Berg and Seemann all played their last games in Scottish football. In the final analysis, it had been a success. Persson had been sold at a profit, Dossing's goals had been valuable and Seemann had been a good servant. Berg's injury problems stalled his contribution but Wing had been an outstanding addition to the squad. In short, the sum of the contribution of the five more than justified the modest investment Kerr had persuaded his board to make.

When it came to an end, the manager refocused his attentions on unearthing home-grown talent. The change in emphasis did not hamper Kerr's own career, with a bumper five-year contract awarded in April 1969 reputedly making him one of the country's highest-earning managers.

In November 1971, half way through that long-term contract, Kerr's tenure drew to a close. Chairman Johnstone Grant called a press conference to break the news that Scotland's longest-serving boss, and the second longest-serving in Britain behind Southampton's Ted Bates, was vacating the dugout.

United had made a slow start to the 1971/72 season and it was decided Kerr would take on a general manager's role to allow fresh blood to lead the team. Kerr declared he was 'very pleased' with the change in role, claiming he had done his part by establishing United as a top-flight force. Few would argue against that point of view, with the enigmatic boss making his team a respected force in among the big boys. Indeed, the chairman intimated that it was Kerr who had offered his resignation and the club which talked him into staying in a revised capacity.

The appointment of Jim McLean in 1971 hailed the brave new era, with Kerr remaining in tandem with the headstrong young coach for two years with his general manager's hat on.

He finally left at the end of the 1972/73 campaign, resurfacing in Angus in September 1974 when he was appointed manager of Forfar Athletic after a spell scouting in Scotland for West Bromwich

Albion. He spent two years with the Loons before standing down, frustrated by the restraints of part-time football on a shoestring budget after the comparative luxury he had enjoyed while in charge at Tannadice.

He left a great football legacy in Dundee; he saw the club through promotion, into European competition and from black and white into tangerine. He also oversaw the Viking invasion of the early 1960s and for the United faithful who had the pleasure of watching Dossing and his cohorts in action that was one of the great blessings of the Kerr reign.

Kerr's name will forever be linked with Tannadice thanks to the decision to rename the original main stand in his honour in 2003. Dossing does not have a stand, but does have a place in the Dundee United hall of fame as one of the seven inaugural members of the distinguished club when it was formed in 2008. He joined Doug Smith, Jimmy Briggs, Dennis Gillespie, Maurice Malpas, David Narey and Paul Hegarty when the magnificent seven were inducted in 2008 and he made the trip across the North Sea to be there on the night. The hall of fame members had been decided by a combination of votes from supporters and the input of the selection panel, with Dossing to date the only continental player from the vast number to have performed at Tannadice with varying degrees of success to have made it onto the roll of honour. The great Dane was a breed apart and remains a popular visitor on his regular appearances back at the ground where he thrilled tens of thousands of supporters.

His name can also be seen from time to time on the banner created in his honour by the supporters' club bearing his name as a small but devoted group from the west coast do their bit to keep a hero of the past linked to the club of the present.

Kilcolm added: 'The supporters club began back in 1994. There was a group of us in Argyll who were United supporters but not season ticket holders and that meant it was very difficult to get seats for the Scottish Cup final. We realised that if we were properly affiliated as a supporters club that we would have a better chance of getting tickets and decided to make it formal. For me there was only one man we could possibly name the club after and the Finn Dossing Argyll Arabs were born.

'I have a season ticket now and travel through for most home games. We take cars rather than a bus and can do the trip in well under three hours. The club also does its bit to bring Dundee United to us. In the summer after the Scottish Cup win in 2010 there was a squad through to play in Oban during pre-season and Keith Haggart from Tannadice brought the Scottish Cup through. We got the chance to get our hands on the trophy and when you consider we've only won it twice, it's quite a big deal. It was great to see a club working with its fans. We have a membership of around fourteen or fifteen ranging from early twenties in age to me at sixty-one. Obviously a lot of the younger ones had never heard of Finn Dossing, let alone seen him play – but they know all about him now.'

1969-1985
HAMISH McALPINE

Magic Moment: In front of the nation's media in 1985, McAlpine collected his Scottish Player of the Year Award to confirm his place as one of the country's finest ever goalkeepers.

Tangerines Career: Games 677. Goals 3.

ONE MAN set the benchmark for Tannadice's love affair with eccentric goalkeepers down through the years. That man was Hamish McAlpine, or Hamish the Goalie as he will forever be immortalised thanks to the wonder of song. McAlpine, a Dundee United legend and cult hero rolled into one incredible package, combined brilliance with entertainment in a way that no other shot-stopper has managed to emulate in almost three decades of trying.

He was the penalty-taking keeper with a penchant for excursions from his box that set hearts racing and had supporters peeking out from beneath outstretched fingers as the sanctity of their goalmouth flashed before them. Yet his brilliance was in equal measure to his audaciousness, as his place as one of only four goalkeepers in the near half century history of the Scottish Football Writers' Association ever to have won the cherished player of the year title from the nation's sporting press illustrates.

McAlpine not only captured the imagination of journalists but also of the supporters who handed over their hard-earned cash at the turnstile every week hoping to be well rewarded. With him on the pitch, they knew there would be value for money as for this exponent of the goalkeeping art the game was about more than simply keeping a ball out of a net. This keeper had grander ideas, aiming to put supporters on the edge of their seats in the same way that a wing wizard or deadly striker could do. McAlpine wanted his own piece of the crowd-pleasing action and, just as importantly, he managed to do that without having to sacrifice the more tangible success that his medals and other football honours point towards.

It is difficult to quantify the love and affection extended from the Tannadice stands towards the club's favourite goalkeeping son, but singer-songwriter Michael Marra has made a good fist of doing just that. It is Marra who penned the song *Hamish the Goalie* and who performs it as part of his set at gigs the length and breadth of the land. The tune, available to download through Marra's own website and other internet music pages, pays tribute to the loveable big player in the Lochee-born song-smith's familiar style. A version was even recorded by Leo Sayer for McAlpine's testimonial in the early 1980s after Marra and Sayer struck up a friendship.

> "If you win a lot you need to be extroverted, or they'll think you're arrogant."
>
> **Alberto Tomba, Olympic skier**

The song, like the man it pays homage to, has stood the test of time. While the Dundee United squad were busy laying down their vocals for the release of *Love is in the Air* in time for the 2010 Scottish Cup final, pupils at St John's High School in the city were also put to work as the second piece of the double A-side jigsaw was put in place – a modern take on Hamish the Goalie. Marra had an input but it was pupil Aoife McGuigan-O'Brien who took centre stage with the lead vocal as the classic lyrics were brought back to life for a new audience to savour as part of a project masterminded by ArabTRUST Board member Colin Stewart through his day job as principal music teacher at the school.

Dundee band The Cundeez, with their tune *Jimmy Gomis* paying tribute to 2010 Scottish Cup winning hero Morgaro Gomis, have continued the proud tradition of immortalising the Tannadice idols in song – but *Hamish the Goalie* will always be the first.

When McAlpine drifted out of the first team at United in the second half of the 1980s, Scottish football became a duller place. It was left to a succession of heirs to the No.1 jersey the legendary custodian had made his own in a career spanning the 1960s, '70s and '80s to try and fill the substantial void created by his retirement.

While McAlpine was gone, he was far from forgotten. It is no surprise that the goalkeepers who have succeeded in winning a place in the collective heart of the Arabs faithful are those who have shown, above all, an ability to entertain.

Billy Thomson, the man who picked up the gauntlet in the immediate aftermath of McAlpine's step back from frontline duty, showed in flashes that he had learnt a trick or two from the old dog. After all, any man who is willing to run out in front of tens of thousands of baying fans wearing tights can hardly be considered a shrinking violet. Thomson's fashion statements extended beyond his leg wear, with his tradition of wearing green to face Rangers and blue when up against Celtic becoming a feature of life on Tayside.

There have been other great characters who have won the affections of their gallery while donning the gloves. Guido van de Kamp, the fiery Dutchman with a heart the size of a lion, ensured his place in the history books when he shut out Rangers in the 1994 Scottish Cup final – and then, in typically stubborn style, promptly returned to the Netherlands to work in a bar after being frozen out of football due to a contract dispute with Jim McLean.

Van de Kamp's countryman Sieb Dijkstra's rashness manifested itself on the pitch rather than off it, with his, at times, unorthodox style causing bafflement and excitement wherever he plied his trade. The moustachioed keeper, whose facial hair in itself was a throwback to McAlpine in his pomp, became expert at interacting with supporters regardless of whether they were home fans cheering him on or away followers barracking his every move. Whether flinging himself forward to clutch at crosses he had no right to be going for or careering from his box at will, there were seldom boring moments with Sieb around. He had arrived at Tannadice in 1996 via an unhappy spell in England with QPR, and then on loan at Wycombe Wanderers and Bristol City, first landing south of the border after a successful period at Motherwell under Tommy McLean. It was McLean, a man not known as one of football's great extroverts, who went back for seconds when he took over at United and signed his former Fir Park keeper for the Tangerine cause. The supporters lapped it up, embracing a new cult hero who evoked a slice of nostalgia for aficionados of the McAlpine style.

Jerry Kerr was first to put his faith in young McAlpine, using him as a deputy to regular No.1 Donald Mackay during the 1968/69 season. The debut ended in a 1-0 defeat against Hearts at Tynecastle and the rookie shot-stopper had to be content with a place in the reserves until the 1970/71 campaign, when he ousted Mackay from the first team two and a half months after the kick-off. From that point on, he never looked back.

Aside from Jim McLean's brief reliance on Sandy Davie in the 1973/74 season, following his return to the fold after a spell in England with Luton and Southampton, McAlpine was the first name on the team sheet throughout the 1970s and into the second half of the 1980s. He had a succession of understudies who attempted to push him out of the side, but McAlpine remained undaunted in the face of competition. He was an ever-present in 1974/75 and the following four seasons in league, cups and in Europe. During that phenomenally consistent run, back-up keepers such as Andy Graham faced a frustrating wait on the sidelines. Graham ended up going out to three clubs on four separate loan deals as he waited for his chance and was just one of a string of young upstarts who tried to compete with McAlpine for a berth in McLean's side.

Even English star Peter Bonetti, himself a character big enough to light up a football stadium, could only temporarily displace McAlpine when he was recruited in a blaze of publicity at the start of the 1979/80 campaign. Bonetti started as first choice but was edged out of the side after just a handful of games, with McAlpine back in pole position in time for the League Cup final replay win over Aberdeen in which he kept a clean sheet.

McAlpine suffered a serious setback in his bid to establish himself as one of Scotland's finest keepers when he endured a calf muscle haemorrhage during an encounter with Rangers in 1980. He was hospitalised for a month as he recovered from the rare injury and required a major skin graft on the wound. He tackled the long path back to full fitness with typical determination and quickly regained his place as United's main man. The injury not only threatened his career but could also have threatened his life had it not been for the prompt medical attention he received.

The 1980/81 season saw him back as an ever-present in all competitions and he was bestowed with the honour of lifting the League Cup when Dundee were defeated 3-0 in the final, with captain Paul Hegarty stepping aside to allow his long-serving colleague the moment in the spotlight. McAlpine himself served as skipper and, despite his reputation as an eccentric, had the respect necessary to fulfil that role. He also had Dundee United at heart and his loyalty never wavered, happy to sign the five-year contracts that were pushed onto the table by the Jim McLean-led regime. Those long-term contracts became a matter of huge concern and equal ridicule, but for McAlpine the prospect of an extended stay at Tannadice was a pleasure rather than a chore.

That is not to say that he did not have his moments of doubt. The relationship between the outspoken goalkeeper and his similarly stubborn manager Jim McLean was a stormy one. Tensions boiled over in the summer of 1979 when McAlpine made the mistake of questioning McLean's tactics during a pre-season tour of Japan. The outcome was a fast plane home to Tayside for the custodian and a spell in solitary confinement to give him time to reflect on the error of his ways. He was fined heavily and banished from the ground, told to stay away until the directors decided what to do with their dissenting star. By that point Bonetti had been brought to Tannadice to provide competition and it looked as though McAlpine had handed the initiative to his rival by falling foul of the boss. It took two months for the dispute to be settled and the air to be cleared, with neither McLean nor his experienced player in the mood to back down.

The key factor was that McLean knew the worth of his increasingly experienced keeper. It was a quality that was crucial to the form in the 1982/83 league-winning season, a year in which McAlpine played every single minute of every match.

By that time John Gardiner was the deputy entrusted with the unenviable task of trying to dislodge the legendary star, who recorded an incredible seventeen shutouts in thirty-six matches on the way to the big prize. Gardiner, who went on to play for Motherwell and then featured as a goalkeeper and a manager in the Highland League, mustered a single appearance in the League Cup while McAlpine kept possession of the gloves with the vigour and enthusiasm that had made him such a hit with supporters in the first place. The fact he played the game with a smile on his face set him a class apart from so many professionals past and present and fans responded to seeing a man who took as much pleasure from playing the game as they did from cheering on their team. His enjoyment was matched by his passion for the United cause.

The goalkeeper was awarded a testimonial in 1983 in recognition of his incredible service to the United cause over the course of three different decades. Tottenham Hotspur provided the opposition and more than 10,000 fans turned out to pay tribute to a true stalwart. The Kilspindie-born lad had first joined the Tannadice side in 1966 and became part of the fixtures and fittings at the club in the 1970s before cementing his reputation with his vintage displays in the 1980s. He had first been spotted playing for junior side North End after earning a Scotland youth cap as a youngster with Butteburn Boys Club. Following his recruitment by the Terrors he was loaned out to Montrose to test him in the senior game.

He quickly developed into a player who was determined, single-minded and confident in the extreme. McAlpine carved out a unique niche for himself as an extra member of the defence, playing as an auxiliary sweeper behind the back four and proving adept at darting from his box to clear up behind his back line. With his confidence on the ball and impressive distribution, the big keeper gave the impression he would not have been out of place in any of the ten outfield positions. In fact he had sampled life as midfielder for United, playing in a reserve game against Motherwell in a game in which he was only denied a goal by the width of the crossbar. Bobby Clark, the Aberdeen keeper of the 1970s and early '80s, is the other notable man to have combined outfield duties with a goalkeeping role but his brief dalliance with life as a central defender for the Tangerines cannot come close to matching his Dundee United adversary's achievements with the ball at his feet.

McAlpine, now in his sixties, exudes warmth and affection when he looks back over his career, speaking with the relaxed lilt of a man content with all he has achieved. According to the great man, his style was organic and never contrived. He told me:

'It really did come naturally to me, I certainly never set out to play a particular way or to do things differently. I enjoyed life and I enjoyed what we were doing with Dundee United at that time, so that came across when I was on the park.

'Although I was a goalkeeper, I liked getting involved in the game as much as I could, whether that was with the ball at my feet or by taking penalties. If you think about it, when you start out playing football at school you play every position – I never lost that type of spirit.

'Playing in goal is unique in the way that you're obviously posted in one part of the pitch for forty-five minutes at a time. There's always shouts from whichever stand you are playing in front of and I didn't mind that all, a bit of banter with the crowd was always a good way to keep things interesting. If things weren't going exactly right for us I would try and get the fans going. I always figured that if the rest of the team heard a cheer going up from our supporters, they would get a lift from that. It was about trying to help the whole team.'

McAlpine was never afraid to step up to the plate and in 1976 he took over as United's penalty taker, having already inherited the captaincy following Doug Smith's retirement. After a miserable run of luck from the spot, Jim McLean turned to his goalkeeper to shoulder the responsibility and he had success in his first attempt as he helped his side to a 2-0 win against Hibs that helped steer the Arabs clear of relegation. He went on to score from the spot against the Easter Road side again the following season and against Rangers at Ibrox – but when he missed from twelve yards against Celtic at Parkhead it marked the end of the experiment and duties reverted to the outfield players. There had been a fright at Ibrox along the way when one of McAlpine's spot kicks thundered off a post and left the visitors scrambling to get back and cover their unguarded net. They got away with it on that occasion and the keeper continued on penalty duty until eventually there was a change in policy to a more orthodox approach. It was left to Andy Rolland to pick up the duties.

McAlpine recalls: 'I remember sitting having a pre-match meal with the rest of the team in Broughty Ferry when the conversation turned to penalties. We'd had a run of missing a few and confidence was obviously a bit low, so nobody was very keen to take the next one. I said that if nobody else wanted to, I'd take on responsibility for the spot kicks. Jim McLean was happy with that and it worked out well enough, I scored far more than I missed.

'The manager had us better organised, more tactically aware and fitter than anyone else in the league, which is one of the main reasons we were so successful, but he also wanted players to express themselves when they went out on the pitch.'

While the excursions from his area remained a feature, McAlpine was left to focus on his duties at the back after passing over penalty duties. He went on to become one of the finest exponents of the art of his generation and in April 1985, at the grand old age of thirty-seven, the goalkeeping king enjoyed his coronation in front of the country's media as he was crowned as Scottish Football Writers' Association player of the year. He was the overwhelming choice for the coveted prize, with two thirds of the press pack placing an X next to McAlpine's name on the voting form. Jim Duffy, then skippering Morton, was runner-up.

The player of the year award was one of the many accolades collected by McAlpine during his illustrious career. The league winner's medal from 1983 was the other most coveted prize and he said:

'For a provincial club it will never happen again. I said after we had won the league in 1983 that it wouldn't, and that has proved to be the case. It hurt Celtic and Rangers to lose the title to us and they were always going to go out and spend big to stop it happening again. You can buy success, but it only leads to problems – as they have found with the money troubles recently.'

The financial drain that has sucked money from the British game in recent years is just one of the factors that worries McAlpine as he assesses football in its current guise. The goalkeeping legend is frank in his opinion about the state of play, claiming:

'It's crap. A lot of football now is absolutely shocking and it is certainly a changed game from when I was playing. The physical side has been stripped away totally and I don't find what is left particularly appealing. Put it this way, I wouldn't give up doing something else on a Saturday to go and watch football.

'The World Cup in 2010 was an absolute disgrace. The players who were there in South Africa want for nothing and the vast majority are millionaires – yet they are falling down like wee lassies in the playground when there's the slightest bit of contact. It is not all down to the players because the rules have been changed so much, but the men on the park have a responsibility as well.

'Football should be a man's game. In our era the last thing you did was go down and let an opponent know he had hurt you. If you had to, you'd get treatment a few minutes later and pretend you'd twisted your knee or something. Goalkeepers now don't know they are born – I got absolutely battered, but I gave as good as I got and never complained. It was part and parcel of the game.

'The players from our team probably wouldn't be able to play now. They would have been booked after ten minutes and sent off after twenty. It has really become a non-contact sport. I wouldn't like to be playing now because the fun has gone out of it, football's become too clinical.'

Clinical is not the way McAlpine played the game, but beneath the extrovert approach to the game was a rock-solid base of technique and instinct that served him so well right through to his veteran years.

The player of the year award in 1985 represented an incredible end to a campaign in which the keeper had started off not knowing whether he would be able to win a place in the team. Jim McLean had recruited Billy Thomson from St Mirren in the summer of 1984 and his arrival was expected to signal the end of the veteran No.1's possession of the gloves. But nobody had bargained on the popular big shot-stopper's resilience and character, with McAlpine coming back stronger than ever and producing the most consistent season of his career. Other rewards for his late flourish included being handed the captaincy of Scotland's under-21 team as an over-age player in the national set-up, although a cap for the full side proved elusive. Given his domestic success, it was staggering that McAlpine was overlooked by a succession of Scotland managers. The Dundee United supporters knew what the Tartan Army were missing out on and given the extrovert nature of the national team's support there is no doubt they would have savoured a helping of Hamish, a man who thought nothing of conducting the Arabs choir in the Shed during lulls in goalmouth action.

The award from the nation's press came as McAlpine was entering the twilight of his career, fitting recognition for a lifetime in the sport as he prepared for the curtain to fall. In the final weeks of the 1985/86 season, as McAlpine's career drew to a close, the experienced campaigner answered an SOS from Dunfermline. He moved to East End Park on loan as the Pars challenged for promotion from the Second Division. Ian Westwater had been struck by a virus and reserve Hugh Whyte was unavailable, leaving McAlpine to step into the breach. It was not a happy venture, with the Fifers falling to a 4-0 defeat against Meadowbank in Edinburgh. He had happier times in Fife with Raith Rovers during a two-year stint at Stark's Park, even scoring the winner with a clearance in a 4-3 win against Kilmarnock at Rugby Park to relive his days as a goalscorer. McAlpine rounded off his playing days with a spell in the Arbroath team in the 1988/89 season.

He had been considered as a candidate for a place alongside Jim McLean on the coaching team at the time when Walter Smith was Ibrox-bound, but it was a career outside of the game that beckoned when McAlpine finally called time on his playing commitments. He entered the licensed trade as landlord at a pub in Dundee before moving into sales and also assisting with commercial operations at Tannadice.

His sporting passions were maintained through golf, which had always been a major part of his life. McAlpine even had the opportunity to try his hand at professional golf while still on the books at Tannadice. As a thirty-something he had been offered sponsorship to turn his back on the beautiful game and try his hand on the fairways. As tempting as it was for a two-handicap player, he decided there was unfinished business in football.

That did not curtail his interest in other pursuits though, with the versatile McAlpine trying his hand at ice hockey, darts, snooker, handball, shooting, fishing and cricket during an eventful career. In cricket, he held the distinction of hitting a century as a budding amateur player.

Golf always remained the main interest and in June 1986 McAlpine became a world record holder when he and Gordon McKay, a former captain of Camperdown Golf Club, completed a twenty-four-hour golf marathon. They played a hundred and one holes over twenty-four hours at a succession of courses across the region after starting at Camperdown and ending the mammoth cross-country effort at McAlpine's home track in Alyth, the club at which he currently serves as vice-captain. The golfing bug has bitten his son, Kevin, who has become established as one of Scotland's leading amateurs, winning the national amateur strokeplay championship at Nairn in 2006.

Kevin has kept the famous McAlpine name to the fore in Scottish sport. If he can go on to enjoy the same success and provide equal entertainment as his famous father did in football, the country's golf fans are in for a real treat.

McAlpine senior said: 'I always had a great relationship with the Dundee United supporters and that has never changed. When I go to dinners or functions I always get a lovely reaction and a few cheers, which is appreciated. It is nice to be paid compliments and for people to remember what you achieved, but it doesn't put money in your pocket. You have to move on with your life.

'We didn't play football because of what we could get out of the game – it was a job you enjoyed. It was great to go into the ground in the morning and have a bit of a carry on, great to work hard on the training pitch and great to run out and play in big games week in and week out. I wouldn't swap what I had for all the money they earn now – I've no regrets at all.'

1974-1989
PAUL STURROCK

Magic Moment: Sturrock knocked home his 168th and final goal in United colours to complete his incredible haul and etch his place at the top of the club's list of post-war goalscorers.

Tangerines Career: Games 566. Goals 168. Caps 20.

WHEN THE BBC conducted a nationwide survey to find the definitive cult hero for each British club in 2004 there was an overwhelming groundswell of support for Paul Sturrock. In the online poll of United fans, he claimed a fifty-eight per cent share of the vote to beat Hamish McAlpine, on thirty-seven per cent, and Craig Brewster, on five per cent, to the title. It may not have ranked up there alongside Sturrock's more heavyweight honours in a glittering career as a player, but the accolade was more than a subtle hint at the popularity the talismanic star had, and still retains, among the Tannadice supporters.

Sturrock is the man who defined a generation. His goals in crucial games were the catalyst for so many of the notable successes of the Jim McLean era and his remarkable devotion to the cause was admirable. Flying wingers and goalscorers, those most precious of football commodities, have traditionally not been able to resist the lure of big-money moves and the ego-massaging trappings of that fame. Sturrock was a different animal, a refined and level-headed attacker who loved scoring goals and making goals for the fans who adored him and had no inclination to seek greener grass on which to ply his trade.

Since hanging up his boots to concentrate on coaching, the man who had previously been considered a homebody has developed a wanderlust that has taken him from Perthshire to Devon, to Hampshire, Yorkshire, Wiltshire and, in his latest role as boss at Southend United, the Essex coast.

It could be viewed as making up for lost time, having been one of the game's rare one-club men as a player. Sturrock, however, insists he has no qualms about his decision only ever to pull on United's colours.

Sturrock told me: 'I had sixteen years with Dundee United and many teams came in for me, but they would never entertain selling. I retired in 1989 – the year the Bosman ruling came into play. I went from four-year contract to four-year contract but never wanted to leave, I've no regrets at all about spending my playing career with the one club – we were like a family. Jim McLean also ran a very tight ship in a business sense, which enabled him to keep the nucleus of the side together and happy.

"The legacy of heroes is the memory of a great name and the inheritance of a great example."

Benjamin Disraeli, British prime minister

'Celtic tried five times to sign me under three or four different managers. Alex Ferguson was interested when he first went to Manchester United and West Ham were another team keen to take me to England. Every time, Jim McLean refused. When Jim was expected to take the manager's job at Rangers, part of the deal was to take myself and David Narey with him – which would have totally shattered the non-Catholic policy at Ibrox.'

Sturrock, speaking during his League Two Southend United's team's journey from the south to the Midlands for a League Cup tie at Wolverhampton early in his tenure with the Shrimpers, said:

'I enjoyed my career and my sixteen years as a player at Tannadice, just as I have enjoyed my fifteen years so far as a manager and the success I have had. It has been a whole new chapter for me and I've had some wonderful times, including promotions with St Johnstone, Plymouth, Swindon and Sheffield Wednesday. Five promotions, and managing in the Premier League in both Scotland and England, is a good return but I am still passionate about the game – I wouldn't be travelling up the road from Southend to Wolverhampton for a midweek game if I didn't have that enthusiasm.'

Paul Whitehead Sturrock was born in Ellon on 10 October 1956. He was educated at Pitlochry primary and secondary schools and played for the junior side Grandtully Vale. In 1972 he joined Vale of Atholl in the Perthshire Amateur First Division where he scored over 100 goals for them in the 1972/73 season. He then moved on to junior football with Bankfoot Athletic, where he continued to hit the back of the net with regularity. After trials with Morton and St Johnstone he was signed by Dundee United manager Jim McLean in the summer of 1974.

Sturrock credits the Tannadice coaching team of McLean and Gordon Wallace with transforming him from a decent player to a great one. He spent hours on end with Wallace on the training pitch working on his weaker left foot, time that paid dividends in the years that followed as he hammered home goals with left and right feet and proved skilled with his head.

The small acorn from which the giant oak grew was a European Cup Winners' Cup tie against the Romanian side Jiul Petrosani in

September 1974, when a seventeen-year-old Sturrock was given his debut as a substitute in his side's 3-0 canter against the men from the east. That was early in the 1974/75 season but it was the tail end of that campaign that brought Sturrock's career to life. He was promoted to the first eleven for the final eight matches of the league programme and in the fifth match of that run he signalled his potential with a double in a 2-2 draw against Rangers at Tannadice. In his next outing Sturrock was again on the scoresheet in a 2-1 win at Clyde and then grabbed the only goal of the game the following week at home to Morton. In the last match of the season a Sturrock double took his tally to six goals in four matches as he helped United to a 4-2 win at Kilmarnock and rounded off a term in which they had comfortably held fourth spot.

The 1975/76 season was the one in which Sturrock played his way into a regular place in the side and by 1976/77 he was a Premier Division ever-present, finishing as United's leading scorer with fifteen strikes in thirty-six league matches. A further goal in the League Cup gave him a total of sixteen, three clear of Gordon Wallace. Goal scoring was only part of the Sturrock game, with his contribution as a provider just as valuable to the cause.

His first international recognition came in that impressive 1976/77 season when he was capped at under-21 level against Czechoslovakia. Sturrock's international career brought him twenty caps – but it could have been far more. Manager Jock Stein once confided in the United star that he would have been first choice had it not been for a certain Kenny Dalglish being ahead of him in the queue for a striking berth.

The United man made his debut in dark blue in May 1981 in a 1-0 home nations championship defeat against Wales in Swansea, introduced by Stein as a late replacement for Arthur Graham. The first of three international goals came just months after his first appearance, in a 2-1 friendly defeat in Portugal, and he made it onto the scoresheet against East Germany in 1982 and then Yugoslavia two years later.

He went on to take his place in the 1982 World Cup squad but had to wait until 1986 to fulfil his ambition to get on the field in the finals, when he was part of Alex Ferguson's starting eleven for the 1-0 defeat against Denmark and the 0-0 draw against Uruguay in Mexico.

At club level, Sturrock had continued to pop up with vital goals at important times, not least his effort in the 1979/80 League Cup final replay which ended 3-0 in United's favour after the first game against Aberdeen had ended deadlocked at 0-0. The initial match at Hampden was played on a Saturday afternoon but the replay was switched to Dens Park on a cold Wednesday evening just four days after the teams had jousted for the first time. There was in fact a bigger crowd inside Dens than there had been at Hampden and the heat of the atmosphere more than made up for the chill in the air, with the occasion helping to spur United on to a far more positive display than they had mustered in what had been their first major cup final days earlier. Willie Pettigrew settled the nerves with a goal after quarter of an hour and when Sturrock swung in a perfect cross for Pettigrew to head home the second on sixty-five minutes, it looked as though Alex Ferguson's men were dead and buried. Sturrock made sure fourteen minutes later when he beat the Dons' defence hands down and ran through to beat veteran keeper Bobby Clark to make it 3-0 and clinch the club's first major honour in seventy years of trying. It was a momentous occasion and fitting that Sturrock, such a devoted servant, had had a hand in the outcome.

He went one better in the final the following season as the trophy was retained, scoring twice in the 3-0 victory against Dundee in a game played at Dens after a coin toss had determined which of the two teams would play host to the showpiece occasion of a derby final. It was a pressure-cooker environment for the cup holders, but they coped admirably with the intensity of the situation and ensured there was no delay in landing the second honour.

It was not all champagne and celebrations during a decade and a half of football in the top flight. Sturrock was on the losing side in the 1980/81 Scottish Cup final against Rangers and again in the League Cup final against the Ibrox men the following term. In the 1983/84 season a leg injury sidelined Sturrock for six months, but he battled back to fitness and form.

However, there were far more highs than lows. When the league title was clinched in 1983, Sturrock was a key man. He played in all but eight of the thirty-six matches on the march to the Premier Division crown and scored eight goals while playing a vital supporting role to leading goal-scoring light Ralph Milne.

Sturrock said: 'As a player the championship win was the highlight. There are very few Premier Division medals that do not have Rangers or Celtic names on them and I'm proud to have one of them. Nothing will ever beat that, it was a special team and a special time for all of us.

'I don't think anyone realised how significant our achievements were, not just domestically but in Europe too. Nobody remembers that we reached the semi-finals of the European Cup, that we led Roma 2-0 going into the second leg and only lost in Italy after a match in which it was later revealed the referee had taken a bribe. For Dundee United to get that close to the European Cup final, to go that distance in a competition normally contested by Liverpool and all of the giants of the continental game was incredible.

'It was a small band of boys who came together under the leadership of a tactical genius in Jim McLean. With Walter Smith and Archie Knox as his coaching staff, we had a strong team on and off the park. It will never be achieved again in Scotland, where the quality has taken a nose dive. There has been a slight improvement and signs of recovery, with several players coming down to England in recent years, but time will tell if that can be built upon.

'It took nine years for the championship-winning side to come together, with so many of us joining as young lads and coming through the ranks. When you consider the back four of Gough, Hegarty, Narey and Malpas were all internationals it tells you so much about the quality we had. Eamon Bannon, such an astute signing, was another international and Ralph Milne should have been. Myself and Davie Dodds also played for Scotland while the others who had a major part in that success were all great players in their own right. It was a team that achieved so much yet probably should have done even more.'

The man from Perthshire returned to the top of the Tannadice scoring chart in the 1984/85 season with his first ever twenty-goal haul in all competitions, which included a run to the Scottish Cup final and a goal against Manchester United at Old Trafford when the Red Devils were held 2-2 by the Terrors in the UEFA Cup. He savoured even greater European highs as part of the UEFA Cup final team in the 1986/87 term, the year in which he was again on the losing side in the Scottish Cup final when St Mirren emerged victorious.

As the 1990s loomed, Sturrock called time on his playing commitments to concentrate on his role as a coach under Jim

McLean. He made fifteen appearances, seven from the bench, during his swansong in 1988/89 before swapping his playing kit for a tracksuit as he passed on the benefit of his years of experience at the top level to the new generation of United players. It appeared he was being groomed for the top job by his mentor McLean, but there would be more twists and turns during his coaching career than either man could have anticipated.

He learnt much from McLean, the man he hails as a tactical genius. When it comes to man-management, Sturrock admits that this is where his approach differs completely from his old gaffer's dictatorial style. Instead, he prefers the softer carrot and stick psychology.

United had to be cruel to be kind as they set Sturrock off on the meandering managerial path which has led him on a series of adventures. Having cut his coaching teeth under Jim McLean, the Tannadice legend looked favourite to succeed his mentor when McLean stood down in 1993. Sturrock was overlooked when Ivan Golac took charge. The decision should have left the Tannadice stalwart devastated but he used it as a spur to go out into the big bad football world and seek the kick-start needed.

He joined St Johnstone in November 1993 as manager, replacing John McClelland following his resignation, and freely admitted he felt homesick after leaving Tannadice, even if it was just a short hop down the dual carriageway to Perth.

In the cold light of day he could see the benefit in severing his ties to Tannadice, admitting that if he had replaced McLean that the club would have suffered by inheriting a clone of the man he had worked for as man and boy. By breaking free he had room to make his own mistakes and learn his own lessons, even though he frequently turned to McLean for advice and an understanding ear.

He was brought in by St Johnstone owner Geoff Brown to steady a ship in danger of sinking. The club had amassed a paltry thirteen points from seventeen games when they turned to their new man, a coach Brown labelled as 'the most promising young manager in the Premier Division' after handing him his first job as a boss in his own right. Brown was quick to point out that the Perth men had missed out on Sturrock as a young player making his way in the game and they were determined not to make the same mistake again.

Fittingly, his debut put him up against old foes Dundee at Dens Park to provide an added spur.

It was a new type of challenge for a man brought up on a diet of success at United. He had to set his sights on more humble targets, with survival the first and foremost aim. The opening fixture ended in a 1-0 victory and the new manager was off and running. Even with the fresh impetus, Saints remained mired in the relegation zone and tumbled out of the Premier Division.

Two years after becoming a manager, Sturrock gave Scottish football a horrendous fright when he collapsed during a return to Tannadice with St Johnstone in October 1995. There was panic in the ground as his players in St Johnstone colours and former colleagues in tangerine could only look on helplessly as medics worked to ease his discomfort. Sturrock's wife, Barbara, rushed from her seat in the stand to be by her husband's side and news of his condition quickly spread through the football world. One by one the well-wishers stood forward to express their concern, a vote of popularity that the patient would rather have gone without.

The Saints boss, suffering from chest pains, was rushed to hospital by ambulance and spent weeks recuperating.

He used his time to reassess Scottish football and his attitude to the game. Rather than coming back and easing himself gently into the swing of things, he returned with a new work ethic to instil in his squad. Gone were the short days and afternoons off; in their place was a nine-to-five regime with an emphasis on ball work and perfection.

He felt sure that more time on the training pitch would help bridge the gap developing between Scottish players and their continental counterparts. For a man who had dedicated his life to the game it was no sacrifice to up the workload and take a new approach and he expected the same enthusiasm from his charges.

It took a few years for the Sturrock blueprint to take shape, but when it did there was significant success. He led his side to the First Division championship in 1996/97 and upon their return to the top flight established them as a force to be reckoned with among the big boys.

It was confident and tangible progress, something that had not gone unnoticed at Tannadice. When the hunt began for Tommy McLean's successor at Dundee United there appeared only to be one direction in which the search party would be heading and it was straight to Perth. It was Sturrock's time, his chance to test himself in the post he appeared destined to occupy from the moment he led his first training session as a rookie coach under the watchful eye of Jim McLean in the 1980s. It was always a question of when, not if, he would become United manager.

The moment came in September 1998, inheriting a team that had laboured to seventh place in the Premier Division the previous season and had failed to win any of the opening four league matches of the new campaign. Three of those had ended in defeat whilst in the League Cup it took penalties to squeeze past Stirling Albion before an embarrassing defeat against Ross County in the next round. McLean was ushered out and Sturrock entered stage right, hoping to once again become the saviour of Tannadice.

Unfortunately history did not repeat itself and the task proved an impossible one. Ninth place in his first season was followed by eighth in 1999/2000, leading to Sturrock's departure to make way for old-stager Alex Smith.

After leaving Dundee United in the summer of 2000 it did not take long for the Tannadice legend to regroup and bounce back. He was tempted back into the dugout by Plymouth Argyle, a club without the same weight of expectation attached to United.

When Sturrock took over at Plymouth in October 2000 they were a club languishing in the lower reaches of the bottom tier of the English game. With faithful sidekick John Blackley at his side, the Scottish duo guided the Devon men to the League Two title and had broken a host of records in the process – including a club and league best of 102 points. By October 2003, Sturrock and his management team had taken Argyle to the top of League One. It was a fresh challenge and one Sturrock attacked with vigour, becoming a hero at Argyle. The Plymouth adventure was about more than just football though, with Sturrock settling into a new way of life on the south coast during his first experience of life away from the goldfish bowl of Tayside.

If he could be accused of making one error at Plymouth it was in leaving for the promise of bigger and better things.

The impressive form prompted Southampton to move in and take the duo along the coast to replace Gordon Strachan in 2004. Sturrock's reign at Southampton was, like the club itself at that moment, a troubled one. He left after just four months.

A month after leaving Southampton he was appointed manager at Sheffield Wednesday, taking them into the League One play-offs and through to the Championship with a win over Hartlepool at the Millennium Stadium in the final. He said:

'The best moment in management was winning the play-off final with Sheffield Wednesday, with 41,000 of our supporters at the game the noise was incredible. We went from one goal up to 2-1 down, before putting on three substitutes and turning it around. It was an amazing atmosphere and to win promotion with a big club like Wednesday was fantastic.'

Sturrock maintained Wednesday's position in the Championship the following season and at the commencement of the following campaign signed a four-year contract. Five weeks later he was sacked. His management services were quickly secured, this time by Swindon Town, and he led the Robins to promotion from League Two.

Just as he was at Dundee United, Sturrock quickly became a fans' favourite at Plymouth, Sheffield Wednesday and Swindon. The English fans have found a place in their heart for the shrewd Scot, who has taken a little slice of Caledonia with him on his travels. He invested in a traditional manor house in Devon but his brand of improvements included a flagpole complete with Saltire fluttering atop.

At the start of the 2007/08 season, with Swindon in the top half of the table, Plymouth came calling. His homecoming was not a happy one, ending with a move 'upstairs' into a behind-the-scenes role after a slump in form.

His return to the frontline with Southend United came in time for the 2010/11 season. In accepting the Southend challenge, Sturrock proved what every United fan already knew: he's a man with the heart for a real battle. Rather than spending time at his Devon country pile and taking time to enjoy the finer things in life as his fifty-fifth birthday loomed, he plunged himself headlong into arguably the most thankless job in the British game as he attempted to rebuild a flagging club from the bottom up with scant resources.

When Sturrock agreed to take charge he was joining a team with just a few first-team players registered for the upcoming campaign. He was joining a team with crippling debts, that had not paid its players for the previous two months as well as having its hands tied by a league-enforced transfer embargo due to the financial problems. He was joining a team facing two winding-up orders and which was still licking its wounds after the ignominy of relegation to League Two. Yet he said 'yes', he would take the job. Glutton for punishment or football's very own crusader against despair, either way he made a brave decision when he signed up at Roots Hall.

He explained: 'Southend have been in the doldrums. When we came in we had four players and just two weeks to find another seventeen. It is always a challenge to get that many new players to gel together and hopefully we can see that through. Unfortunately time is in short supply in football. The average lifespan for a Championship manager is ten months – compare that to the time it took for our Dundee United team to grow into a championship-winning side.'

Even in the face of all those testing circumstances, the new manager claimed Southend United was his kind of club. Perhaps that should be read as a club with a whole lot of character, just like its charismatic coach.

Sturrock, who has put concerns about his health to one side following his diagnosis with Parkinson's Disease in 2000, remains as determined to succeed as he did when he first stepped through the front door at Tannadice more than three decades ago.

He said: 'I've enjoyed every minute of my time in management but I've still a couple of wee ambitions left to fulfil. One is to taste a national team manager's role and another is to coach abroad for a year to sample that. The final ambition is to come back to Scotland and take on the part-time challenge, working with players who are coming to train after finishing work at five o'clock and seeing how difficult that environment is. I would see that as my last stop in management, but there is a lot of work to be done before then.'

DAVID NAREY

Magic Moment: A nation held its breath as the improbable suddenly looked possible. Narey's screamer against the Samba Kings made it Scotland 1 Brazil 0.

Tangerines Career: Games 866. Goals 36. Caps 35.

DAVID NAREY, Dundee United stalwart and Tannadice legend. Can a man with 866 appearances to his credit lay claim to the title of cult hero? For his club he was more than a cult figure, he was in with the bricks and mortar. He was a steady and dependable influence, free of drama or fuss. Yet for country, Narey is the ultimate cult hero. His goal against Brazil in 1982, yes *that* goal, has made the quiet and unassuming Dundonian part of Scottish international football folklore and united the nation with one common purpose: to knock Mr Jimmy Hill from his lofty perch as the sport's unelected authority on the beautiful game.

The chant of 'We Hate Jimmy Hill' became part and parcel of life as a member of the Tartan Army, as the pundit discovered what it felt like to be on the receiving end of the collective wrath of the population north of the border. That passion was stirred on 18 June 1982, the day on which Hill became public enemy No.1.

The Estadio Benito Villamarin in the southern Spanish football hotbed of Seville was the setting for the act that sparked the infamous case of foot in mouth, a moment in time that no self-respecting Scotland fan can fail to remember. The World Cup finals match against the samba kings brought Narey's one and only international goal and it was a thing of beauty. Graeme Souness, prowling the midfield, collected the ball just inside enemy territory and lofted a neat pass forward into the right channel for John Wark to rise and nod the ball down into the path of Narey, charging forward from his right-back berth, to control the ball with a deft left-foot touch before firing an unstoppable right-foot shot past the goalkeeper for one of the finest goals of the entire tournament. He turned, both arms aloft, to be greeted by jubilant team-mates who knew they had witnessed something special under the Spanish sun. Scotland were playing their revered opponents at their own game and were winning.

As the ball rifled into the postage-stamp corner, the hopes of a nation reached fever pitch. Could it really happen? Could Narey's cracker inspire a famous victory? Well, no. Instead it merely irritated the impressive South Americans and they fought back from the early setback to win 4-1. To rub salt into the wound, Jimmy Hill had the audacity to describe *that* goal as a 'toe poke'. It was an off-the-cuff remark designed to irk the Scottish audience – but not even Hill could have predicted the scale of the ire his assessment would provoke. Or, for that matter, the length of time the feelings would burn for. Even now, among fans not old enough to have been born when the United man's screamer ruffled the Brazilian net, there's a universal dislike of a former pundit who has disappeared from terrestrial television. Hill was part of the BBC's team when he made his 'toe poke' claim, settling into a role as an analyst having been credited with inventing the role of the football

> "You'll never have a quiet world until you knock the patriotism out of the human race."
>
> **George Bernard Shaw, playwright**

pundit when he introduced the expert panel for the 1970 World Cup coverage in his position as head of sport for London Weekend Television. He was the godfather of punditry, but didn't always get it right. Not that he was quick to admit his gaffes – it took until 1998, during the World Cup finals in France, for him to apologise to Scotland supporters for his slight on Narey's piece of brilliance.

The 1998 World Cup coincided with the release of Hill's autobiography, a tome which included the pundit's explanation for the incident. Hill said:

'David Narey broke away at the far end of the ground. As he approached Brazil's penalty area it seemed as if the ball had run fractionally too far ahead of him. Nevertheless he shot from well out and scored, sending the Scots into a state of delirium. In describing David's goal I ventured the opinion "It might have been a toe poke" surmising it was the only way in which he could reach the ball to shoot. I went on to say "It doesn't matter how he scored Scotland are ahead of Brazil and perhaps on their way to victory". No one remembered that phrase when Brazil finally won 4-1.

'Of course, I was aware that kids not blessed with football ability tended to kick with their toe rather than their instep. I wasn't accusing David of that, I merely believed that he couldn't have reached the ball and shot so powerfully in any other way. Crest-fallen, disappointed Scots wanted to believe otherwise and have never let me forget it. As they filed past our commentary position on leaving the ground I said "Hard luck!" to one lad. "Have my scarf" he replied and draped it around my neck. "Hard luck!" I said to another. He spat, but unlike David Narey, he missed.'

For the record, even Socrates, Brazil's captain on the day, has vouched for the quality of Narey's wonder strike. When the World Cup legend met the then Prime Minister Gordon Brown in Sao

Paulo in 2009, ahead of a G20 summit, the conversation naturally drifted to *that* goal. Brown's reference to the 'toe poke' assessment in the aftermath of the 1982 game drew a wry smile from his host, who in turn described it as a 'very good goal'. For a man not alien to a special strike, it was an opinion carrying great weight. So that settles it, the 'toe poke' was indeed a strike to cherish.

Almost thirty years on, the goal remains up there with the most famous in Scottish history. Only Archie Gemmill's memorable meander through the Dutch defence in 1978 and, in more modern times, the James McFadden belter against France in Paris in 2007 come close to matching it for sheer impact.

The goal was classy but Hill's crass putdown was not. Even now the sense of injustice about that putdown is putting fire in the bellies of Scotland fans. For Dr Lawrie Spence, the 'toe poke furore' has become part of his football life. The Highland doctor, when not engrossed in his medical career, can be found at his keyboard as one of Scottish football's growing band of devoted internet bloggers.

His site's name harks back to an event that took place even before Spence, now in his mid-twenties, was born: *nareystoepoker. blogspot.com.*

Spence said: 'Most people enjoy the name and know exactly what it's all about. The only problem I've had with it was when two presenters of an English podcast dedicated to looking at different football blogs chose to focus on mine one week. They called to clarify the title and make sure they were pronouncing it right, so obviously Narey's toe poke was new to them. It must not be part of the English psyche in the way it is here in Scotland.

'I'm only twenty six, so barely old enough to have seen David Narey play football let alone to have seen the goal. I wasn't even born when he scored it, but I must have seen it a thousand times on different programmes. Initially I came up with the nareystoepoker name for a fantasy football team and the blog followed from there. There have not been too many goals as special as that for Scotland supporters to celebrate. Obviously there was Archie Gemmill's one against Holland in 1978 and James McFadden's long-distance strike against France – but in so many ways the Narey goal against Brazil was the perfect Scottish goal. Not only was it brilliant, but it was part of a glorious defeat in which Brazil scored four just as good as his. When you watch it back, it really was a wonderful goal that any striker would have been proud of. The fact it came from a defender made it all the more remarkable.

'The aftermath appealed to the Scottish mentality, the fact that a truly great goal was derided by an English media pundit. The fact the Jimmy Hill chant can still be heard at some Scotland games tells you everything you need to know about how that comment went down. Quite often you see compilations of World Cup goals and Narey's is part of that. How many Englishmen are on those packages? Not many that I can think of.'

The good doctor's tribute to Narey's screamer does not hint towards a Dundee United leaning. Like United fans he has a love of provincial football and a passion for the underdog, born out of his love for the SPL's youngest club.

He said: 'I'm stuck with Caley Thistle I'm afraid. I was brought up on Highland League football and taken to Kingsmills to watch Inverness Thistle with my dad. The Old Firm were to be hated, although my dad did have tenuous loyalties to Aberdeen. I think it was a case of having a team different from everyone else he went to school with to support. After the merger of Thistle and Caley in Inverness, I was taken along to Ross County for two years in protest. I started going along to Caley Thistle games just as the shiny new stadium was in place and the team was heading for promotion. I've been a season ticket holder for five years now.'

Blogging has become one of football's boom sectors, with a succession of sites springing up to allow anyone and everyone with an interest to have their say through the medium of their own online column.

Spence's musings have attracted a loyal following, although he admits the blog is purely a recreational pursuit rather than one with the commercial slant that other blogs have adopted. He said:

'I started the blog in 2007 and one of the very early subjects was Scotland's win against France in Paris. I was working in the accident and emergency department in Aberdeen at the time over a four-month period. I obviously had a lot of evening and weekend shifts, totally opposite to most of my friends. That left me with plenty of spare time when everyone else was at work to work on the blog.

'Initially I thought I would write mainly about Caley Thistle, but it soon broadened out to cover all things Scottish. I like the idea of having somewhere I can vent and it's also a good way of sparking discussions with friends who, because of the age I'm at, are scattered in various locations. They read the blog and are ready to jump on anything they don't agree with.

'The time I have to spend on the writing comes and goes, depending on my shifts. I try to write at least once a week, although there have been long periods in the past where it just hasn't been possible. Because it's a purely amateur effort and mainly for my own amusement, there is no big obligation on me to meet any deadlines or come up with a set amount of copy. I am in the middle of general practice training and by the time the new season is underway will be off to work in GP, so I'm looking forward to having my Saturdays free to get back to football regularly and to get food for thought for *nareystoepoker*.

'People like the name, it touches a chord with most people who have any affection for the Scottish national team. I always feel we are looking for someone to accuse for our own failings. When Narey's goal was not enough to beat the Brazilians, it somehow became Jimmy Hill's fault. It ties in with the chip on the shoulder that every Scottish football fan has to have to support the team.'

Narey's goal against Brazil gave the Tartan Army strength to believe, coming on the back of the team's convincing 5-1 trouncing of New Zealand in the opening group game of the World Cup finals in Spain. The subsequent Brazilian backlash, and 4-1 defeat, left the hopes of passing to the knock-out stage hanging by a thread and the 2-2 draw against the USSR in the final pool match snapped that thread.

It was a disappointment for Jock Stein's men but the tournament had been something of a personal triumph for Narey, who played in all three matches and set about establishing himself in world-class company.

He had first been capped as a twenty-year-old in April 1977 when he was drafted in by Willie Ormond to play in a friendly against Sweden at Hampden. It made him the first Arabs player to pull on the dark blue jersey. Over the next four years he won a further nine caps, but it was in the build-up to the 1982 World Cup that Narey finally began to emerge as a cornerstone of the dark blue cause.

After his sterling efforts in Spain, Narey eventually became a fixture in the Scotland side and went on to serve with distinction in the 1986 World Cup finals in Mexico under Alex Ferguson. He featured in the 2-1 defeat against West Germany and 0-0 draw with Uruguay, on his way to thirty-five appearances between his debut in 1977 and final outing against Cyprus in 1989 as part of the successful qualifying campaign for the 1990 World Cup finals in Italy.

The World Cup in Spain was a dream tournament for Narey, even before his most memorable moment on the international stage is factored into the equation. He played in all three of Scotland's matches and looked destined for a long and fruitful career in dark blue.

But the game is nothing if not unpredictable. Narey disappeared from the national team scene in the wake of the finals, sent into a three-year exile despite playing his part in United's incredible rise to prominence during the first half of the 1980s.

Rumours in football circles suggested Narey had been bombed out after expressing displeasure to manager Jock Stein about being asked to turn out at full back rather than in his more recognised central role. Narey was at pains to dismiss those claims in later years, insisting his omission was as much a mystery to him as it was to the Tannadice fans who could only watch in bemusement as squad after squad was named without Narey in its number. Having won twenty-five caps in the six years after bursting on the Scotland scene in 1977, he became a victim of circumstance as much as anything else. Willie Miller and Alex McLeish at Aberdeen had edged ahead of the Narey and Paul Hegarty partnership at Scotland level and that pairing proved difficult to shift.

Ironically it was Alex Ferguson, club manager of Miller and McLeish at Aberdeen, who brought the stopper back into the fold, recalling him for a friendly against Israel early in 1986 as the build-up to the World Cup finals in Mexico began in earnest.

He had served under Ormond, Stein, Ferguson and Andy Roxburgh during a period in which the country was not short of defensive talent. Tam Forsyth and Gordon McQueen were among the stoppers being utilised when Narey was first blooded. His tenure in dark blue also coincided with the service of McLeish and Miller while former Tannadice team-mate Richard Gough provided another obstacle. It led to appearances at right back for Narey due to the plethora of players competing for the central defensive deployment that would undoubtedly have served him best. In familiar fashion, he set about his business in an efficient and committed manner and never failed to give his all for the Scotland cause. In fact it was his versatility that led to his initial international recognition.

He had first been involved in the Scotland fold as far back as 1974. Narey was signed by United as a youngster from Dundee amateur outfit St Columba's and wasted no time in making an impact. After joining Dundee United he was quickly promoted to the Scottish professional youth side, putting his powerful 6ft 1in frame to good use in amongst his fellow teenage prospects. Scotland manager Willie Ormond took note of the imposing young player and included him in his under-23 squad at the tail end of 1974.

Narey had been blooded in the Tannadice side by Jim McLean as a midfield player, kept out of his preferred defensive position by the experienced trio of Doug Smith, Walter Smith and Jackie Copland.

McLean's masterplan was to ease him into the first-team fold in the middle of the park before giving him the added responsibility of a defensive berth – but even at that early stage, the manager had no doubt about the talent of his protégé.

Speaking with the New Year bells of 1975 still ringing in his ears, McLean damned his new boy with faint praise when he said:

'He is a bit lazy and has to be forced to work, but he has a lot of class and I rate him as highly as Andy Gray, who has been attracting leading English clubs. This boy has a great future – and it will be at Tannadice. He has tremendous potential, skill, toughness and class.'

Even at that stage McLean was resigned to losing Gray, who was United's top scorer by that point, to the lure of the bright lights and big bucks of the English game. But with Narey he sensed he had a player who was an Arab for life, a born and bred Dundonian whose ambitions revolved around making his home-city club a force to be reckoned with.

In addition to needing a gentle nudge to increase Narey's productivity on the park, McLean's aim was to bring more toughness to the teenager's game. It all fell into place with perfect results as he grew to become a dependable and rugged cairn at the centre of the Tannadice defence.

Not surprisingly the defender with the bright future was not short of admirers, but the interested parties, mainly from south of the border, were given short shrift by a manager intent on building a side around the unfussy talents of his new face.

He made his debut in a low-key encounter on 21 November 1973, pulling on the No.6 jersey to take the place of Pat Gardner after McLean had shuffled his pack. Falkirk were the opposition at Tannadice and, in front of a crowd of just 1,302 people, Narey was introduced to first-team life at the age of seventeen years and five months in a 2-1 victory against the Bairns. That season he was gently eased into the fray, dipping in and out of the side until getting a run of games under his belt in the closing weeks of the campaign.

At the start of the 1974/75 term it was all change. Narey had gone from young prospect to become one of the first names on McLean's team sheet, taking over the No.6 jersey previously worn by the steadying influence of Walter Smith. With Smith nearing the end of his career and Doug Smith also beginning to wind down, there was room for the new kid on the block to stake his claim for a permanent place. Nobody could have guessed just how permanent that would be, nor the extent of the loyalty Narey would show to the cause in the years and decades ahead.

He was a vital cog in the United machine as it moved from mid-table respectability to a position of being able to challenge the Old Firm. Narey and his team-mates finished third in the 1977/78 campaign, a hint at the great strides that were about to follow.

The Dundonian was an ever-present in the League Cup campaign in 1979/80 that culminated in United lifting the trophy after a 3-0 replay victory against Aberdeen at Dens Park and again played every single tie the following year when the cup was retained with another 3-0 win, this time against Dundee, in the final.

That joy was tamed when later in the 1980/81 season he suffered the pain of losing to Rangers in the Scottish Cup final, with the ignominy of a 4-1 replay defeat after a gallant 0-0 draw in the first game.

Rangers also defeated Narey and his side in the final of the 1981/82 League Cup but that disappointment was confined to the dustbin when the following year the ultimate prize was claimed: Dundee United were Premier Division champions, Scotland's finest.

Hamish McAlpine, the legendary Paul Hegarty and Narey were the three men who played every minute of all thirty-six league fixtures in that momentous campaign, the rocks upon which greatest success in the club's 100-year history was built. They we. at the heart of a defensive unit that had a steely resolve as well as an enormous amount of class and ability, with the Hegarty and Narey partnership regarded as one of the finest double acts the domestic game has ever seen. During that triumphant season they conceded a miserly thirty-five goals in thirty-six matches, helping the Terrors to a proud record of just four defeats in the entire league programme. Almost 30,000 were crammed into Dens Park for the final game of the season as Ralph Milne and Eamon Bannon's goals clinched a 2-1 win and sparked a night of wonderful celebrations in the City of Discovery.

It proved to be the pinnacle of Narey's career, not least because he had scaled the incredible heights with his hometown team. Few on the outside had gone into the season believing United could knock dominant Celtic off the summit of the table but McLean's drive instilled a confidence in his team that anything was possible. United's glory, followed soon after by Aberdeen's own taste of championship success, ensured the 'New Firm' were the new words on everyone's lips.

With the Dons lifting the European Cup Winners' Cup in 1983 and United storming through to the semi-finals of the European Cup the following year, narrowly losing out to Roma 3-2 on aggregate in the final four, the pecking order had changed completely. Oh how the Arabs in the stands enjoyed that.

The only blackspot remained the Scottish Cup, with defeat in the 1985 final against Celtic followed by defeat against St Mirren two years later, making it third time unlucky for Narey. In between he had featured in the team defeated 1-0 by Rangers in the 1984/85 League Cup final. Narey appeared in his fourth Scottish

Cup final in 1988 with what was by then a familiar outcome, United losing 2-1 to Celtic on that occasion. He missed out on the fifth Scottish Cup final defeat, the 4-3 thriller against Motherwell in 1991, and by the time the prize was finally lifted in 1994 the veteran defender was a bystander. That 1993/94 season proved to be his last as a key member of the Tannadice squad, playing his last game in a 1-0 win at Hibs in February 1994 in what was one of a handful of appearances he made that term before moving on to Raith Rovers for a short spell across the Tay Bridge.

Prior to his retirement the Narey medal collection grew when he travelled to Buckingham Palace in November 1992 to be honoured by the Queen. Narey was presented with an MBE in recognition of his services to football over the course of twenty years with United. He was thirty-six by that point, but still going strong. The gong took pride of place next to his Premier Division prize from 1983 and League Cup winner's medals from 1979 and 1980. Nobody will ever be able to take those honours away from the Tannadice legend – just as nobody will ever be able to erase that fabulous goal against Brazil from the memories of the Tartan Army.

1976-1986

DAVIE DODDS

Magic Moment: Scottish football's biggest prize was heading for Tannadice for the first time and the hometown boy was at the heart of the party.

Tangerines Career: Games 367. Goals 150. Caps 2.

NEVER HAS singing in the rain been quite so appealing for diehard Arabs as it was in May 1983. The rain was pouring and lightning was striking, but the thousands who took to the streets of Dundee that night did not care a jot. They had congregated to welcome their championship-winning heroes and braved unseasonably hostile weather to be able to say: 'I was there.'

A crowd estimated to be in the region of 5,000 had gathered at City Square and on the steps of the Caird Hall, with the flag- and banner-waving masses spilling into Reform Street for the men who had clinched the precious first Premier Division championship in the club's history. There was a carnival atmosphere as the team arrived on an open-top bus, with officials presumably not expecting the monsoon conditions they were greeted with.

"Just singing in the rain, what a glorious feeling..."

Gene Kelly, actor

The rain could not dampen the spirits among players and supporters alike with Davie Dodds, resplendent in the giant top hat he had commandeered when the honour was clinched at

Dens Park the previous day. It was not quite a crown to mark the day United became kings of Scotland, but it did the job just as well.

Dodds, still a young man at just twenty-four when the trophy was paraded ahead of United's civic reception, had good cause to milk the celebrations. As a hometown boy he had achieved what many, including his manager Jim McLean, had not even dared to dream of. Into the bargain, he had done it in style as the main man in the most successful team ever to grace to Tannadice. It was a perfect case of the local lad who lived the dream.

His contribution to that most memorable of years cannot be underestimated. Dodds weighed in with twenty-two Premier Division goals during his run of featuring in every one of the thirty-six fixtures, two of which came from the bench. Only Paul Hegarty, Hamish McAlpine and David Narey shared the distinction of playing in each and every match.

A hat-trick against Morton was among the highlights for Dodds but he also recorded vital singles, including the match winner against Dundee in the first derby of the season and another in a 1-1 draw against Celtic, proving his appetite for the big occasion. He scored twenty-eight goals in all competitions and was emerging as one of Scotland's deadliest strikers as well as a hero to the United support, who had taken to heart one of their own. The fact he was so often derided and mocked by opposition supporters made that bond even stronger.

Dodds was recruited by McLean in 1975 after starring in youth football in Dundee, having started off on the road to stardom while a pupil at Dens Road Primary School. He was capped by Scotland's pro youth team before being fast-tracked through the United reserve side and into McLean's top squad. From those early days he was marked out as a player with enormous potential thanks to a mix of athleticism, aggression and the type of goal-scoring instinct that cannot be coached.

It was only a matter of time before he graduated and was eased into the fray in a League Cup group game at Arbroath in August 1976. The seventeen-year-old responded by scoring twice at Gayfield in a 3-1, playing in three more ties in the opening weeks of the season before dropping back down to the second string to continue his football education outside of the intense glare of the Premier Division spotlight.

The 1977/78 campaign saw Dodds used sparingly again, loaned out to Abroath for a spell early in the season after the Red Lichties had been hit by an injury to key striker Jimmy Bone as they competed in the First Division. Perhaps McLean was in sympathetic mood, having hammered the Angus side 4-0 just days earlier in the League Cup, but more importantly the loan stint represented another part of the McLean master plan for turning a promising young goalscorer into the finished product, ready to challenge for a place in his starting eleven on a week-in week-out basis.

By the time the 1978/79 season began the process was complete and young Dodds, capped at under-21 level by Scotland in 1978, was ready for his elevation, pushing his way forward from the bench after some sparkling cameo displays to establish himself as the man in possession of the No.9 shirt by the time the curtain fell. United had led the league for long periods that term, but fell just short of championship form after two defeats and a draw in the last four matches. The flipside was that Dodds had scored five times in the closing half dozen fixtures and was primed to play a big part in the years ahead. Whilst others had found the step up to the big-time too hard to handle, there was no question that Dodds had the attitude to thrive at that level.

The 1980/81 season completed the rise and rise of Davie Dodds as he equalled Paul Sturrock and became the joint golden boot winner at Tannadice with his twenty-three goal haul across all competitions. That impressive tally included a hat-trick at Airdrie in the league and another treble against Motherwell in the Scottish Cup. Dodds popped up with another Scottish Cup goal in the final against Rangers, though not enough to prevent a 4-1 defeat. By then he already had his first winner's medal in the bag after opening the scoring against Dundee in the League Cup final at Dens Park to set up a 3-0 win and ensure the trophy remained at Tannadice for another year. Dodds had not played in the previous year's final win but had time to make up for that.

The following term the Dodds and Sturrock partnership again proved one to count on, with the youngster bagging twenty-two goals and Sturrock notching twenty-four. The tables were about to turn and the championship-winning season of 1982/83 was a fitting time for Dodds to try on the leading goalscorer's crown for size.

It was not only Jim McLean who rated the developing Tannadice talent, with Jock Stein, then in his Scotland capacity, also enticed by his physical presence and impressive goal return. It was on the back of a burst of goals in tangerine and black that Dodds got his Scotland break in September 1983. After his heroics in the championship success the previous season, Dodds was quickly into his stride when the 1983/84 campaign began. A double against Hibs and then another goal against St Johnstone the following week thrust him into Stein's plans, as the manager searched for reinforcements to counter a spate of call-offs for a friendly against Uruguay at Hampden. Although the twenty-four-year-old Terrors star was on the bench, an injury to Frank McGarvey ensured he got to play in the lion's share of the match against the rugged South Americans. Dodds was introduced after just seventeen minutes and handled the big occasion as well as he could possibly have expected. Within seven minutes of Dodds appearing on the scene, Nottingham Forest's John Robertson had put Scotland ahead. Ten minutes after the half-time break it was the turn of Dodds to put his name of the scoresheet, completing a 2-0 victory and a satisfying start to life in the colours of his country.

Dodds and Richard Gough were the only two members of the Premier Division-winning United squad to play for Scotland that night – despite the fact the club had achieved that remarkable milestone with an entirely homegrown group of players. The talents of the Class of 1983 were undoubtedly overlooked and underestimated, with Dodds showing the strength of character to force his way into the reckoning when the odds were stacked against him and his United club colleagues. It could not even be claimed that west coast bias was responsible, since Aberdeen had a string of players called up for international duty during the same period.

The bustling forward retained his place in Stein's pool as the European Championship qualifiers drew towards a conclusion against Belgium at the national stadium the following month, although it was Charlie Nicholas and Kenny Dalglish who got the nod to start against the Belgians and Frank McGarvey who provided the support from the substitute's bench.

The new recruit from the east coast was drafted in for the home International fixture against Northern Ireland at Windsor Park in December 1983, a game that provided him with his first start for

Scotland but also proved to be his last run-out for the national side. Dodds was used as the foil to the prolific McGarvey and also partnered Aberdeen's Mark Ghee in the second half of that encounter as Stein searched for the perfect pick from a healthy crop of young and energetic attacking players who each brought their own qualities to the mix. It was the same wealth of options that restricted Paul Sturrock's involvement in dark blue and ensured that Ralph Milne's talents were never displayed on the biggest stage of all, but Dodds at least had the opportunity to get his hands on two caps and sample life in the Scotland fold. It was another achievement in a career at the top that brought honours that many of his peers were not fortunate enough to savour.

At club level, Dodds remained top of the scoring chart for the club in the 1983/84 season and the vultures began to circle. Perhaps it had been his accomplished displays in the memorable European Cup run that drew attention to the unfussy forward, with Dodds at the centre of the run to the semi-finals of the competition. He was one of seven men who played in all eight of United's ties in the continent's biggest club competition that term. He scored in the 4-0 rout of Standard Liege but more importantly was on target in the quarter-final second leg against Rapid Vienna on Tayside. His team needed a 1-0 win to progress after a 2-1 reverse in Austria – and a left-foot belter from Dodds secured safe passage. It was Dodds who opened the scoring in the 2-0 victory over Roma in the first leg of the semi-final to give hope of an upset that was close but so agonisingly far, a dream shattered by the now infamous 3-0 tumble in Italy.

Although the 1983/84 season ended without a trophy, it had been an eventful and successful campaign for Dodds. He had won his first cap, played a starring role in European football and continued his good scoring form. Reports of interest from across Scotland began to surface and in the summer of 1984 the player requested a transfer, a demand reluctantly accepted by his club. Liverpool had previously expressed an interest but it appeared Aberdeen and Celtic were the more likely employers.

His future remained undecided when the 1984/85 campaign began but in October 1984 Celtic attempted to prise United's star man away from the east coast, lodging a bid that was instantly dismissed by Jim McLean. The situation led to a furious war of words between the two clubs, with the Parkhead side accused of trying to unsettle Dodds by leaking their interest to the press after the initial offer had been rejected. The success McLean and his side had enjoyed had not surprisingly brought admiring glances from elsewhere and Celtic were among the most persistent suitors of the brightest young talent at Tannadice. The Arabs stood firm and refused to be bullied into selling, despite Celtic's claims that they had offered what would have been a record fee between two Scottish sides to try and secure the services of Dodds. The Hoops board later lamented the fact that a bounty of £300,000 had not been enough to persuade McLean to back down. In the end Dodds remained in tangerine and black, playing on the losing side when the Hoops went head to head with the Terrors at Hampden in the Scottish Cup final at the end of that term.

Dodds settled back into life as United player for the next season, but by the time the team embarked on its run to the UEFA Cup final in the 1986/87 season he was long gone. In March 1986 news emerged that he had taken advantage of transfer regulations to open secret talks with Swiss side Neuchatel Xamax as he played out the final months of his Tannadice deal. Neuchatel had knocked the Arabs out of the UEFA Cup months earlier and obviously liked what they saw in Dodds. As they prepared for European Cup football, the continental outfit stole a march on all of the other interested parties with their covert operation. Not even McLean knew where Dodds was heading, only informed that his protégé was destined for a European side. The manager did not appreciate the cloak and dagger negotiations and at one point banned the striker from Tannadice in the wake of the confirmation of his intentions to sign a three-year deal in Switzerland with weeks of the Scottish season still to play. United's anger was not tempered by a decision that the fee should be £180,000 – well short of the £300,000 valuation the club had initially placed on a player they had reared for eleven years. He had recently joined Frank McGarvey and Derek Johnstone in passing the century mark in terms of Premier Division goals, putting him up there with the best in the Scottish game, and United believed they had a good case for a sizeable fee. That was of little concern to Dodds, who had decided two years previously that he would not renew his contract after being upset by the club's decision to reject Celtic's bid and the fact a previous offer from Liverpool had not been mentioned to him.

The fee the Swiss side had to pay was determined by a formula which dictated out of contract players could move to the continent for a sum roughly equivalent to eight times their annual basic salary. For once, McLean's legendary thrifty nature and reliance on excellent bonuses to top up wages would not pay dividends. But money was really only a secondary issue in the Dodds transfer saga. More than anything it was the loss of control that irked the manager, who was powerless to play any part in the dealings and did not even have contact from the buying club until the process was more or less complete. It was the first time Dundee United had lost one of their crop of rising stars to a European club in that fashion and represented a frightening glimpse into the post-Bosman ruling future. Whereas now football clubs and supporters have come to accept the principles of free movement that Jean-Marc Bosman fought so hard to have introduced in the game, in the 1980s it felt like midnight robbery to lose a player with little or no say in what his new club would have to pay for his services.

Even though the transfer was entirely above board and within the existing framework laid down by UEFA, it hurt to be losing a young Dundonian in that manner. Newspaper reports of the time suggested that it was not just the management and supporters who viewed the imminent move with suspicion – his team-mates were also reported to have shown their displeasure towards their exiting colleague during a painful 3-0 reverse at Hearts in the closing weeks of his time in tangerine. It was after that game that Dodds was told he had played his last game for the club.

McLean claimed: 'This is not a case of victimisation. It is simply one of carrying out now what many thought might have been carried out before this. It was really important, when the news of his impending transfer came out, with the programme we faced, not to disrupt the squad further.'

McLean's comments after the Tynecastle disaster hinted that he was ready to concede the championship to Celtic after a gallant battle with the Parkhead men, not that he would ever admit that directly. The reverse against the Jambos had been a crushing blow and it was Dodds who bore the brunt that day as the hopes of another league flag began to fade.

There were still four games remaining in the campaign to try and salvage the season, but in those games there was no place for the striker. He was banished from even training with the first-team squad and was replaced in the league run-in by Ian Redford. A draw against Clydebank and defeat against St Mirren provided the final nails in the title coffin and McLean's side had to eventually settle for third spot at the end of a season that had contained the usual fireworks on and off the field. While the Arabs squad regrouped for another tilt at the league, Dodds was packing his bags to try his luck in foreign climes. Neuchatel had offered a bumper deal, including a luxury house and car, to tempt him abroad but at the back of his mind Dodds must have considered it a short-term adventure. He kept his house in Dundee and his wife remained in Scotland as he tested the water in Swiss football. It transpired his instinct to keep roots in his homeland were right.

The Swiss adventure turned into a nightmare for the Dundonian, who was left kicking his heels on the sidelines by French coach Gilbert Giresse. His troubles soon filtered back to Scotland and Walter Smith, who had coached Dodds at Tannadice, was swift to alert his new employers, Rangers, to the forward's availability. Aberdeen manager Alex Ferguson was also an admirer and it was the Dons who won the day. By then twenty-seven, Dodds arrived in the north-east in September 1986 to pledge his future to Aberdeen and get his career back on track. He had cost £215,000 but Ferguson believed it was a bargain, citing his new man's strength as well as his will to win as the main qualities he had invested in. Ferguson also raved about the professionalism of Dodds. He had a very strong record of putting the ball in the back of the net too, which was another of his key selling points for a club desperately trying to maintain their place as one of Europe's finest. Having been in the same position while down the A96 at Tannadice, it was not a challenge that fazed the tall and athletic frontman.

Just as he had done on his United debut, Dodds scored on his first appearance for the Dons in a friendly against Brechin City. It was the start of a four-year contract but the long stay at Pittodrie was cut short half-way through that deal when Dodds, after two injury-hampered years, requested a transfer. A change in management, from Ian Porterfield to Alex Smith, led to a change of heart as he heralded the arrival of Smith as a new beginning for Aberdeen after the disappointment of Porterfield's tenure.

West Brom, Sunderland, QPR, Motherwell and Hearts had all been interested but for the man who grew up supporting the Ibrox side there was only one decision to make when Rangers came calling in 1989.

He joined Graeme Souness in a £125,000 deal in the summer of 1989, a move that surprised even Aberdeen manager Alex Smith as the thirty-two-year-old prepared for his big break late in life. Souness had missed out on his target three years earlier but that did not deter him from returning for a second attempt, seeing the worth in a very experienced former Scotland international who did not carry the same high profile as the bulk of his big-money buys but would prove to be a valuable squad man. Kevin Drinkell was on the brink of a move to Coventry and his planned replacement, Gary McSwegan, had broken his leg in a reserve game. Dodds was the man who answered the SOS from Ibrox.

Although used sparingly, he spent two years in and around the first team at Ibrox before retiring from playing to concentrate on coaching commitments with the Light Blues. Dodds was part of the Rangers coaching team for six years under his one-time Tannadice mentor Walter Smith. Dodds carved out a good reputation as a reliable coach during that period and when he departed Ibrox as part of Dick Advocaat's overhaul of the staff he was short-listed for the Canadian national team's manager's job. That move did not materialise, with Dodds instead returning to familiar territory in Dundee to work outside of football at the end of a career which had taken him on some extraordinary adventures.

He went from wannabe schoolboy to championship-winning hero, from Scotland star to Tannadice outcast and from continental transfer pioneer to Old Firm saviour. It was a long and winding path but it was Dundee that was home to his greatest sporting triumph and the city where he will always be part of football folklore.

1979-1986

RALPH MILNE

Magic Moment: Nerves? What nerves? Milne was the coolest customer in the ground as his delectable lob in the final league game of the 1982/83 season put United ahead against Dundee and on the road to the League Championship.

Tangerines Career: Games 285. Goals 74.

THE WORLD of sports books has become a veritable literary maze in recent years, not least when it comes to football tomes. In days gone by it was simple. Superstardom equalled autobiography, maybe. Bobby Charlton and George Best were the benchmark. Then came the explosion as the lines between football and showbusiness blurred and the public demand for celebrity memoirs shot through the roof. With demand from the public came demand from publishers for suitable subjects and the net was cast far and wide. It was open season for old pros everywhere as the boom years rolled merrily on.

"A great book should leave you with many experiences, and slightly exhausted. You should live several lives while reading it."

William Styron, author

Slowly but surely reality began to kick in. Supporters had had their fill and started to become picky. In turn publishers have had to become choosy to ensure expensive mistakes are avoided and that means the once wide net has been narrowed considerably.

The English Premier League, with its hype and glitz, has become something of a microcosm for an entire industry. Just as with wages and transfer fees, the stakes have been raised and gambles have been won and lost in spectacular fashion. The twin moral to the football story has been that fortune does not necessarily follow fame and that celebrity should not necessarily be confused with popularity.

The *Guardian* put the whole spectrum of high-profile auto-biographies under the spotlight in an intriguing investigation headlined 'I'm famous, buy me' in 2007. The newspaper high-lighted the success stories, including the phenomenal sales of Peter Kay's book and those of Terry Wogan and Gordon Ramsay, as well as some of the disappointments which brought headaches to publishers who had shelled out big money to secure the likes of Michael Barrymore and Chantelle Houghton of *Big Brother* infamy but were rewarded with paltry sales in the thousands.

In football, the starkest contrast can be found in old London town. Ashley Cole, at the height of the publicity generated by his marriage to woman of the moment Cheryl Cole, was hooked on a bumper contract earning him hundreds of thousands of pounds before a word of *In My Defence* had even been written. The publisher banked on the Cole factor to get tills ringing and on the publicity machine to set tongues wagging and help sell the book. In the end Cole's book is reported to have sold just 4,000 copies in the aftermath of its high-profile launch. His complaints of his meagre Arsenal salary of £55,000 per week did not help him connect with the man in the street, not entirely surprisingly. Needless to say, it was not a profitable exercise for the publisher. Perry Groves on the other hand was apparently a roaring success. The initial outlay for the publisher who saw the potential in the former Arsenal hero, of a 1980s vintage, was a fraction of that showered on Cole yet the sales outstripped the contemporary London footballer many times over. And there, in a nutshell, is every publisher's dilemma. As in horseracing, there is no such thing as a safe bet. A string of mainstream publishers baulked at the idea of spending big to lure Katie Price to their stable; instead it was a bargain-basement deal that she eventually had to commit to in order to get her story told. And when it was told, it sold more than a million copies and made both her and her grateful publisher a sizeable windfall. The book business is indeed an inexact science and fortune can favour the brave as well as the sensible.

The process for any autobiography begins months, if not years, before the finished article appears on the shelf. The first step is the proposal, the all-important document designed to show the potential in the subject. The next stage is getting that proposal accepted and agreeing a contract that appeals to both parties and then the fun can begin as the story is shaped, perfected and brought to its audience.

For those first crucial hurdles to be overcome, in the increasingly risk-conscious business climate, there has to be a consensus that the personality in question has the strength of character to captivate and engage the readership. Step forward Mr Ralph Milne. For many outwith the Tannadice catchment area the name may not merit more than a flicker of recognition. Even for United supporters of a younger vintage than the man himself, the player in question may have been a mystery. But to Black & White Publishing, Milne was an individual who ticked all of the prerequisite boxes.

Popular beyond modern perception during the club's most successful period, Milne carries the added attractions of controversy and intrigue. As his own book, entitled *What's It All About, Ralphie?*, highlights, the path to and from stardom has not run smoothly. He found himself falling out of love with Jim McLean and in love with the familiar hard-living lifestyle that has lured many great players before and since.

That covers controversy and Milne's disappearance from public life following his playing career takes care of the intrigue. The problem with telling the story of anyone who has enjoyed even a modicum of fame in the digital age is coming up with a tale that hasn't already been told, chewed over and spat out by the incessant media machine of the modern world. That problem can be magnified ten-fold if the subject is still in the path of that machine as pundit, columnist, coach or manager. Milne was not, in fact even the most ardent Dundee United aficionado would have been hard pushed to tell you where his post-football days had taken him.

The answer was to Bristol, where he ran a pub for several years before moving back to Dundee in more recent times and beginning work on the book which has put him squarely back in the limelight.

Just as his tome had hooked a prominent publisher, it also pulled in readers in their thousands as the traditional Christmas rush kicked in at the end of 2009. Crucially, the release also had the newspapers interested as Scotland's press rediscovered one of the stars of the eighties with a nostalgic passion.

Its release coincided with a notable lull in Scottish football. Clubs had crashed out of European competition left, right and centre while hopes of a place at the 2010 World Cup for the national team had been dashed and there were genuine fears that the domestic game was ready to implode as the near-catastrophic impact of the global financial meltdown hit hard. In times of need the tendency was to look to the past for inspiration, to pull on the rose-tinted spectacles and stare fondly back to a time when Scotland's teams puffed their chests out and held their own against the best in Europe. During Milne's era the sides leading the way were Alex Ferguson's bolshy Aberdeen men and Milne's own Dundee United outfit. For a press pack worn down by the monotony of Old Firm dominance, the opportunity to pore over the days when title races included the young upstarts from the New Firm was just as appealing as the prospect of those happy memories of the '80s' successes on the continental stage.

Milne was a willing interviewee as he adjusted to his return to frontline media action and the fact he had such an enticing story to tell made sure the questions flew thick and fast. How did his relationship with McLean end? Why did he leave his beloved Dundee United? When did he discover Manchester United were ready to throw him a lifeline? All those topics and many more were covered during a flurry of interest in the story brought to the fore by the publisher behind the life story of Chic Charnley and Graham Roberts amongst others. A taste for characters is clear in the Black & White stable, with a leaning towards players who captured the heart and soul of the crowd they played to. In short: cult heroes.

For all his self-confessed weaknesses, a lack of confidence was never something Milne could be accused of suffering from. When he was just eighteen years old he pushed his way past more established players to earn a place in Jim McLean's squad for the 1979/80 season and the manager clearly had no worries about his ability to handle the big occasion. His first appearances came in the relative sanctuary of the League Cup, still in its sectional format, against Airdrie. After two outings against the Diamonds the teenager was deemed ready for the big one – Celtic at Celtic Park. Milne came on from the bench to score the goal that secured his side a 2-2 draw against the Hoops after Willie Pettigrew had also made it onto the scoresheet.

He scored again against Hibs at Tannadice just weeks later and was well on the road to becoming an established star. He had more than belief – he had an exciting style and ability to pose a threat every time he had the ball. With pace to burn as well as skill to beat a man, in Milne the McLean conveyor belt of youth talent had produced a Dundonian gem to savour and cherish. His at times bewildering skills were mated to an audacious range of finishing, with his goals spanning everything from scorching long-distance volleys to the most subtle of lobs. Surging runs from deep were a speciality, with the ball appearing glued to his boot as he weaved through panicked defences faced with the terrifying sight of Milne heading towards them in top gear.

Milne was not part of the League Cup-winning side in his maiden campaign or the 1980/81 term, although he did feature in the Scottish Cup final replay defeat against Rangers in 1981.

The 1981/82 season saw Milne finally earn his spurs as a bona fide first-team player, missing just a handful of league games as well as featuring week-in week-out in the domestic cups and the UEFA Cup, adventures that included yet more Hampden disappointment in the shape of the 2-1 defeat against Rangers in the League Cup climax. Milne's goal in that game was not enough to prevent the Ibrox men sneaking a 2-1 victory and leave him still searching for his first winner's medal.

That came in 1982/83 when he was one of the standout players in the Premier Division winning squad. In thirty starts and four substitute appearances he scored an impressive sixteen goals – including a string of vitally important ones on the home stretch.

In the final half-dozen matches of the season he scored the decisive goal in the 3-2 win against Celtic at Parkhead, another in the 4-0 win at Morton a fortnight before the end of the campaign and then the first in the 2-1 win against Dundee at Dens on the last day of the term that guaranteed the league flag would be fluttering proudly above Tannadice. That goal on enemy territory was a thing of beauty, poetry in motion as he raced clear of his marker before sending a perfect chip over the head of Dark Blues goalkeeper Colin Kelly from twenty-five yards to send the Tangerine section of the 29,000 crowd into raptures. It was typical Milne: while all around him were tense and nervous as the title lay on the line, he was a vision of calmness and had the presence of mind to produce the type of finish that would be fit to grace any ground.

Other highlights included his presence in every tie leading to the semi-final of the European Cup against Roma in 1984 as he became something of a specialist in the continental game. There was also another Scottish Cup final appearance, albeit in a 2-1 loss to Celtic, the following year.

As the years passed Milne's right to a place in the starting eleven faded, but his lack of regular first-team football did not prevent Alex Ferguson from taking an almighty gamble on the United man in the years ahead.

His at times volatile relationship with McLean, the man who had mentored him since his youth days, had reached breaking point and Charlton Athletic offered an escape route. Milne has always maintained he never wanted to leave Tannadice but McLean made it untenable for him to stay. Like others before and after him, Milne began to feel as though the only way forward was for him to make a clean break and the Charlton proposition offered exactly that.

His time in London was not a roaring success, but his life was about to take a sudden and dramatic twist. Having moved from Charlton to Bristol City in 1988, there was a call to say Manchester United were interested. And when that happens, there is only one outcome.

Milne moved to Old Trafford in a shock £170,000 move, a shock even to the player at the centre of it. He thought his glory days were behind him, having enjoyed success at Tannadice, but had former Dundee boss Archie Knox to thank for his dream move to the 'Theatre of Dreams'. Knox and Ferguson had watched as their Aberdeen team of the 1980s had gone toe to toe with Jim McLean's Dundee United and more often than not Milne had been a thorn in their side. With United looking for extra attacking impetus as Ferguson assembled the beginnings of his all-conquering dream team, they turned to Milne after Knox had sowed the seed in his manager's mind. The Dundonian went from obscurity to a spot in the Old Trafford dressing room in the blink of an eye. It was a surreal signing in so many ways, with Ferguson still finding his feet in the English game and clearly intent on falling back on the Scots he knew so well from his triumphant days at Pittodrie. Over the years he relied heavily on Gordon Strachan and Brian McClair and had hopes Milne would rise to the challenge in the same fashion and be inspired by his new surroundings and immense possibilities afforded by a club of the size of Manchester United.

It was a hit-or-miss moment for Ferguson and, unfortunately for the manager and his new recruit, it proved to be the latter. Milne played just a handful of games for the Red Devils, mainly in an alien left-wing role as Gordon Strachan was picked for his preferred beat on the right flank, and struggled to take advantage of the big break. Ferguson recently claimed Milne had been his worst signing as a manager, but given his contribution to the Tannadice title win in 1983 you could argue McLean might be inclined to list the same player among his best recruits had it not been for the bitterness that existed between the pair by the time he left his native Tayside behind. McLean might claim that Milne wasted his natural talent by failing to apply himself fully to football and falling into the game's drinking culture in the 1980s and 1990s – but the man in question insists he has no regrets about the way his life and career panned out in his post-Scottish days.

No regrets is perhaps bending the truth. Milne, for all his goals and all his ability, never made it into the Scotland team when he was at his peak in the early 1980s. His belief is that he was only omitted from the 1986 World Cup squad on McLean's advice to Alex Ferguson. Given Ferguson later signed him at club level, his theory that the manager himself was an admirer perhaps carries some weight. While several of his Tannadice colleagues travelled to Mexico to play on the biggest stage of all, he stayed back on Tayside and spent the summer working in a factory to earn extra cash. He played the game in an era of modest returns, even for the best in the business, and it is reasonable to predict that had he been playing in the modern era he would have pocketed millions. His key benefit was the fact that he offered the type of skills that simply cannot be taught. Milne was an instinctive footballer with an ability to take advantage of the smallest of openings in an opposing defence. His speed over the ground, whether with the ball at his feet or not, made Milne a dream to play with and a nightmare to come up against.

Milne, now ensconced back on home territory in Broughty Ferry, released his life story in 2009 and did not hold back in his account of the ups and downs on both sides of the border. He collaborated with writer Gary Robertson on the project, a fellow Dundonian who could relate to his subject's rise to prominence. Robertson himself enjoyed fame when he won the reality television series *SAS – Are You Tough Enough?*. He has also taken to the stage as a poet and musician and performed on radio.

Having that sounding board was vital, helping to bring together a life story that was waiting to be told. The fact Robertson could empathise with Milne with a warmth and integrity born from his own life in Dundee was an important factor in the partnership that worked together with purpose and passion, bringing it to fruition with honesty and with the understanding that readers demand to be entertained.

The market for sports books is notoriously fierce and the swathe of biographies on the shelves means only the fittest survive. Milne, with his tales of excess and memories of the glory days at Tannadice, had the ingredients necessary to stand out from the crowd and add fuel to the all-important fire of publicity. For Milne, who insists talk of his drinking and gambling has been vastly exaggerated, it was also an opportunity to set the record straight regarding his relationship with McLean and to recap on his Old Trafford experiment.

It is a tale of daring and of doing, a story of hope and of despair. Above all else, it is the story of one of Tannadice's best-loved sons and a stirring portrait of a man who thrilled a generation.

1979-1981
WILLIE PETTIGREW

Magic Moment: Two cup final goals from the Pettigrew collection ended the long Tangerines' trophy drought as United were crowned League Cup winners in 1979.

Tangerines Career: Games 91. Goals 36. Caps 5.

IT TAKES just one flash of a muddy boot to turn a great team into a legendary one. The date that happened for the Jim McLean-inspired Dundee United side was 12 December 1979 and the man in possession of that all-important piece of footwear was Willie Pettigrew. He stayed on Tayside for just two years but for an entire generation of Arabs he was the star who instigated a seismic shift in football's grand order.

Until Pettigrew struck his League Cup-winning double against Aberdeen on that night, the glorious twelfth, there were two generalisations. One was that Dundee were the City of Discovery's trophy-winning establishment and the other was that the Old Firm held an almost divine right to dominate the Scottish game. In an instant, as he crashed home the opener against the Dons, both of those misconceptions were blown away and McLean's promising band of men set off on a course that would see them take the Tannadice crowd on an incredible

> "I've learned that people will forget what you said, people will forget what you did, but people will never forget how you made them feel."
>
> **Maya Angelou, author**

journey to the summit of the domestic scene and to previously unthinkable European heights.

Pettigrew, a true two-season wonder with United, was not around to experience the rush of league success in 1983 or the anticipation of the continental challenge in 1987, but he was there at the beginning when the first trophy in seventy years was delivered to the loyal Arabs.

One way or another the 1979 League Cup final was going to represent a changing of the guard in Scottish football. Aberdeen, having beaten both halves of the Old Firm on their way to the showdown with their north-east rivals, were the favourites by virtue of their tough passage to Hampden.

United relished the role of underdog and after the 0-0 draw in the final they got the bit between their teeth in the replay at Dens Park with a performance full of passion and desire. Pettigrew, with his speed and attacking instinct, epitomised that spirit and got his reward when he scored the vital opening goal.

The record books show the final replay ended 3-0 in favour of McLean's team but it was the first goal in that hugely significant encounter that was the most important. It would have been fitting if it had been a goal of great beauty, a World Cup-worthy wonder strike. But it wasn't, and it didn't matter one little bit. Instead it was a typically Scottish goal that set United on their way to their first piece of silverware.

On a dirty winter's night at Dens, Paul Sturrock's left-wing cross landed at the feet of the ever-alert Pettigrew in the Aberdeen box. As he swung his trusty left foot at the incoming cross, the ball plugged in the thick mud inside the penalty area and for the briefest of moments the chance looked lost. Then came the second attempt, this time with the right boot, and this time the connection

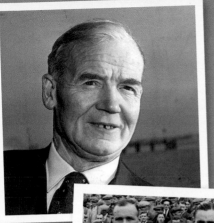

Duncan 'Hurricane' Hutchison went from star player to director at Tannadice.

Neil Paterson (pictured second from right in the front row) was a proud United captain.

Walter Carlyle, in full flight while he was at the peak of his powers as one of Scotland's flying wingers in 1962.

Finn Dossing, pictured in action against Dundee in 1965, had power, poise and determination to make him the perfect striker.

Hamish McAlpine, pictured in action against Dundee during the championship winning 1982/83 season, showing typical flair.

Forfar attempt to keep Paul Sturrock at bay in 1984, a man who has gone from prodigious young player to wily manager during a successful career on and off the park.

David Narey, in action against St Mirren at Tannadice in 1979, went on to become part of Scottish football folklore.

Villie Pettigrew, in action against St Mirren in
1980, is the man who turned Dundee United into
trophy winners in an instant.

Ralph Milne, pictured in 1983 against Celtic, was an entertainer and
goal scorer in one intriguing package during United's glory days.

Davie Dodds, pictured in 1983, was the goal king during the glorious run to the league championship that year.

The powerful John Clark surges away from his Celtic opponents.

Dave Bowman has become a man of many talents in his new guise as a coach, community ambassador and former players club coordinator for the Arabs.

A young Mixu Paatelainen in United colours following his move to Scotland.

Mixu Paatelainen rises to power in a header against Aberdeen, his future employers.

Victor Ferreyra shows a touch of latin flair to keep the ball from Rangers defender David Robertson at Tannadice in 1992.

Scottish Cup winning hero Ivan Golac tries on the prize for size.

Caribbean star Jerren Nixon in action for United in 1994.

Craig Brewster skips past another Dundee challenge during his
rich run of goal scoring for his boyhood heroes in 1994.

Kjell Olofsson, on cup semi-final duty against Kilmarnock in
1997, mated power and presence to a natural attacking instinct.

Scotland under-21 star David Goodwillie on the ball against Falkirk at Tannadice in 2009.

Talismanic striker Jon Daly celebrates after hitting the net against the Bairns early in 2010.

was sweet as the shot flew past Bobby Clark in the Dons' goal. It was 1-0 to United and there was no way the success-starved side were going to let go of that precious lead.

The first goal had been important and the second was decisive. Again it was Pettigrew who delivered, heading home brilliantly from another pinpoint Sturrock cross in the second half to ease the tension and let the celebrations begin in earnest. Sturrock got his name on the scoresheet to complete an impressive 3-0 victory and send the Arabs into raptures.

Almost 29,000 people were crammed into Dens that evening and for the tangerine and black contingent it was the night a new hero was born. Yes, he had scored goals prior to that dramatic cup tie. None would ever come close to matching those two for sheer impact and historic importance though.

Motherwell is the town of Pettigrew's birth and the home of the club with which he made his name, becoming a Well legend during a long and prolific period of service with the Steelmen. While Fir Park fans quite rightly lay claim to him as their own hero, he will forever have a place at Tannadice as the man who turned United into winners. He had only been at the club for four months when he achieved what the United players of the previous seven decades had tried so gallantly to do.

Pettigrew's arrival in the summer of 1979 was big news. When John Bourke was recruited from Dumbarton in 1977 he became United's big-money man; the £60,000 fee was a club record and viewed as a signal of Jim McLean's intent to push the boat out in his determined attempt to put the club on the map as a winning outfit. Within two years that blockbusting fee had been blown out of the water and it was Pettigrew who took on the mantle in August 1979 when he became not only the most expensive United player in the club's history but also the first Tannadice recruit to carry a six-figure price tag. Bourke had not lived up to his star billing, but there was great expectation that the next big signing would.

McLean paid exactly £100,000 to tempt Motherwell to part with their lauded striker. By his own admission, Pettigrew had gone stale at Fir Park and viewed the move to Tayside as an ideal opportunity to rediscover his goal-scoring touch. It was a lock, stock and barrel switch since McLean's strict policy that all players must live in close proximity to Tannadice ensured all new faces had to up sticks and head to the Dundee area.

Injury had restricted Pettigrew's contribution to the Well cause for the best part of two years but both the manager and player were confident the good times were about to roll again. Celtic were of the same opinion and had also made advances towards the striker before being beaten to the punch by United. The Hoops had an offer of £100,000 plus a player swap rejected in March 1979 when the Fir Park board claimed their man was worth double that, leaving Parkhead manager Billy McNeill frustrated. Within months the Steelmen had relented and clearly decided the £100,000 mark was a reasonable one.

It is hard to imagine that Jim McLean did not call upon his brother for a second opinion when he moved for the key target. Willie McLean had been in charge of Motherwell between 1975 and 1978 when Pettigrew was really making a name for himself as one of Europe's leading lights and the manager was impressed by his dedication to the profession. Within months of being installed as Well boss, he had decided to insure his star man for £250,000. It cost the club an annual premium of £2,400 but they felt it was worth protecting their prize asset. A year later he signed a new and improved four-year contract as the Motherwell powerbrokers tried to ward off the growing line of potential buyers. At that stage he was described by Willie McLean as 'the best chance taker around'. Coming from a man who rarely gave much away publicly, it was high praise indeed.

It was Willie McLean who handled negotiations when German clubs began to circle, with Bayern Munich among the clubs who attempted to lure Pettigrew across the channel. Bayern failed in their bid to convince Motherwell to sell but fellow German side St Pauli did manage to strike a £300,000 deal with the Well board in the summer of 1977. The newly promoted side could not agree a package with Pettigrew, who decided against the venture into the Bundesliga, and the then Well manager McLean insisted he was delighted that his most potent attacker would not be making the move. The bean counters may have thought otherwise, although there was still the potential for a lucrative sale into the English market at that stage as scouts from south of the border continued to beat a steady path to the Fir Park door.

A year earlier there had been offers from Manchester City and West Brom, both in excess of £100,000, which had been turned down flat. Arsenal were the other English team who had been alerted to Pettigrew's potential. Motherwell were looking for serious money, the type of cash that could be the difference between a club surviving and being bankrupted at that time. There had been concerns that he was neither fast nor robust enough to withstand the rigours of the English game, that he was purely a penalty-box poacher. But those worries did not prevent teams from pursuing him, with the ratio of nineteen goals in twenty-one games during the 1974/75 season proving to be a considerable draw. He surpassed that the following term to reinforce his position as an extraordinary prospect.

Pettigrew had first arrived at Motherwell from junior football, signing for the Steelmen in 1973 after bouncing back from the disappointment of being released by Hibs in 1972 after failing to make the breakthrough at Easter Road. He went on to combine football with work as a chartered accountant, continuing in that profession even after establishing himself in the Motherwell team.

Within a year of signing for the Lanarkshire team he was a fixture in the Motherwell side and finished as Scotland's leading striker with a twenty-six goal haul. He retained the golden boot the next year when he bagged twenty-nine goals.

Pettigrew continued his club scoring form onto the international stage with Scotland's under-23 side, with highlights of his time in dark blue including doubles against Wales and Romania after bursting onto the scene in the mid-1970s. He had been capped at all age groups up to that stage, adding to the set when he was called up to face Sweden in 1975 by Willie Ormond.

He completed the set when Ormond promoted him to the full international side in April 1975 for a friendly against Switzerland at Hampden Park. Pettigrew was one of five new faces in the experimental side but he stole the show, making an immediate impact when he scored what turned out to be the only goal of the game after just ninety seconds of his international debut. Given he was playing alongside Kenny Dalglish, Derek Johnstone and Andy Gray that day, it was no easy task to edge into the limelight.

The game marked the first of Pettigrew's five Scotland caps in an international career that lasted one year. Remarkably every single one of those appearances ended in victory for Ormond's team, making it all the more baffling that Pettigrew failed to add to his cap collection.

He had scored on his first appearance against the Swiss and also netted in his second game, a 3-1 win against Wales at Hampden in which he opened the scoring for the men in dark blue after thirty-nine minutes, before goals from Bruce Rioch and Eddie Gray secured victory in the home international series.

His other contributions to the national team cause came in a 3-0 win against Northern Ireland at Hampden in the same competition and then as a late substitute in a 1-0 win against Wales, again at home, in the World Cup qualifying campaign for the 1978 finals. The fifth and final appearance was in April 1977 in a 3-1 friendly win against Sweden at Hampden. Five caps, five wins and five matches at Hampden. It was a short, sweet and quirky adventure for a player who was in his early twenties.

As interest from far and wide intensified, the young Pettigrew once claimed: 'I've been scoring goals ever since I put on a pair of boots. I've tried to analyse it, but never came up with a real answer. Call it part-knack, part-instinct. I just accept I can do it and am thankful. If I was to get hung up on the reasons I'd probably dry up.'

His talents were many and varied. Primarily it was his ability to sniff out a chance and his impressive conversion rate that set him apart from his peers but he also had the rare quality of being comfortable shooting with either foot. Add to the mix a razor-sharp striker's brain, blistering pace akin to that of a sprinter and a powerful shot that appeared at odds with his lean frame, and the package was clearly a comprehensive one.

It was that alluring combination of qualities that persuaded Jim McLean to loosen the purse strings and dig deep to secure the services of a proven striker. His two full seasons on Tayside were incredibly eventful. Pettigrew made his first competitive appearance in the Dundee derby that served as a mouth-watering appetiser for the 1979/80 Premier Division season and, despite not scoring, he played his part in a 3-0 victory at Tannadice. His first goal was at Parkhead in a 2-2 draw against Celtic, when he netted from the penalty spot and from then on the distinctive name regularly appeared on the United scoresheet. In fifty appearances in the league, domestic cups and UEFA Cup he scored twenty-two times to finish as the runaway top scorer at the club that term.

Hibs, the team who deemed him not good enough to make it as a youngster, were among the sides who bore the brunt of the new boy's hot scoring form. He netted in each of the four league encounters with the men from Leith, helping his side to a clean sweep of victories. Despite the efforts against the Hibees, it was his exploits against the team from closer to home that had the Arabs well and truly onside. Pettigrew had been on target against Dundee in the Premier Division in December 1979 but it was his display against the Dark Blues in the Scottish Cup the following month that captured the imagination – with a stunning four-goal salvo, including one penalty, helping to dump the Dens team from the competition as, aided and abetted by a Paul Sturrock goal, the Terrors terrorised their neighbours during a 5-1 trouncing at Tannadice.

By that time he had of course proved his credentials as a knock-out specialist with his run of goals in the League Cup that started with one against Queen's Park in the third round and continued with another against Hamilton Accies in the semi-final, to add to his famous double against Aberdeen in the final replay.

The 1980/81 season proved more testing as Pettigrew started less than half of the Premier Division matches and struggled to find the same form in front of goal, only just making it into double figures across all competitions. He did, however, still have a big role to play in retaining the League Cup, having scored the opener in the semi-final second leg against Celtic at Parkhead to put the holders on course for another final appearance as they motored towards a 3-0 victory. He was there in his familiar No.9 shirt for the final against Dundee to make it two winner's medals in two seasons as a United player.

He started the 1981/82 campaign firmly in Jim McLean's plans, scoring four goals in the first nine matches of the season, but was shipped off to pastures new in a shock move before the season got into full swing.

The cup-winning hero's departure was confirmed in September 1981 when Hearts completed a £180,000 swoop on Tannadice, reeling in Pettigrew and fringe player Derek Addison. While Addison, who had come through the youth ranks, was an unknown quantity, Pettigrew was a major loss as far as the Tannadice faithful were concerned. He was still only twenty-eight when he was sold and should have had his best years ahead of him after an impressive start to life in tangerine and black.

Manager Jim McLean admitted at the time: 'It may be a controversial deal, but the players here are paid on a par with any in Scotland and this will ensure that this situation continues. It's a particular blow to lose Pettigrew at this stage but we simply could not afford to refuse that kind of money.'

Fittingly, the big-money deal was brokered in Monte Carlo, where United were posted on UEFA Cup duty against Monaco at the time. The bounty for Pettigrew and Addison swelled the 1981 transfer profits to £250,000 after a series of more minor deals during the course of the year. It gave McLean the budget to keep the rest of his squad happy and reflected the shrewd policy that became a trademark of the successful years. By sacrificing a major player on a regular basis, money was brought in to keep the nucleus of the squad at any one time in place by providing the capital to fund bumper bonuses for the core group. It was an astute, if at times harsh, method of running a football club and one that worked impeccably for many years. It was not until the advent of the Bosman ruling and the inflated salaries of the 1990s that the business model began to struggle to keep pace with developments in the game.

In the 1980s it was perfect, even if it did mean stars had to be sacrificed. Pettigrew was one of the chosen few who had to be sold for the common good and it did not prove to be a beneficial move for the Lanarkshire lad, who became one of the game's forgotten men after drifting into the Tynecastle reserves.

In February 1984 the striker, who had been on loan at Morton from Hearts, made a permanent switch to Greenock when the Cappielow club spent £10,000 to secure the services of a man who had been one of Scottish football's hottest properties just a few years previously.

He had been sent out to 'Ton two months earlier. He was thirty by that time and had been languishing in the Tynecastle second string when Morton boss Tommy McLean snapped him up on the back of his goal-scoring exploits during his peak years. It ensured he had played for all three of the McLean brothers at one point or another and he didn't let any of them down. With Morton he was instrumental in the First Division championship win just months after signing.

More recently Pettigrew has been back in the game as a youth coach and scout, returning to Motherwell in 2004 to work with the Fir Park youngsters and also helping out Dundee United in a similar capacity. Jim McLean was one of his coaching influences, crediting the Tannadice boss as one of the men who helped improve him as a player, and it is clear the short time he spent on Tayside made a big impression.

Pettigrew has since reflected on his time at Tannadice and claimed that Hamish McAlpine and David Narey were among the finest players he ever featured alongside. A third Tannadice player also made it onto his list of all-time greats and that name was, to outsiders at least, less predictable. Graeme Payne is the man in question, the player who thrilled the Arabs crowd for periods during the 1970s and early 1980s. Payne, crowned the Scottish Professional Footballers' Association young player of the year in 1978, had the skill to light up a match and was a hero in his own right for a particular generation of fans. Pettigrew and Payne may not be up there on the hall of fame list but for those who worshipped them from the terraces there can be no doubting the impact they had.

1982-1993
JOHN CLARK

Magic Moment: Under the Spanish night sky, United's Herculean stalwart helped put the mighty Barcelona to the sword.

Tangerines Career: Games 330. Goals 33.

FOR A generation of Dundee United supporters there are two goals above all others that remain etched in the mind. Both came beneath the sprawling stands of the Camp Nou in Barcelona and the first of that memorable double was from the head of the towering John Clark under the Spanish moonlight as the giants of Barca were humbled by their guests from Scotland. It was Clark's bullet header in the UEFA Cup quarter-final against Barcelona on 18 March 1987 that put United back on the path to the final of the competition and his Herculean efforts on that evening in the Catalan capital ensured he was on track for an everlasting place in the files of Tannadice heroes.

United of course went into the away leg against the men in blue and red with a one-goal advantage thanks to Kevin Gallacher's match-winning salvo on Tayside two weeks previously. It always looked likely to be too slender a lead to defend when Jim McLean's likely lads travelled to the continent and that proved to be the case when Barcelona levelled the tie at 1-1 on aggregate just minutes before the half-time interval at the Nou Camp. The travelling supporters were silenced as the dream of causing a major upset began to slip from their grasp and the home fans raised the decibels as they began to look towards another tilt at European glory.

What the 40,000 or so Barca supporters hadn't accounted for was John Clark, the powerhouse of the United team. When he galloped forward to meet a deliciously inviting left-wing free-kick there was only ever going to be one outcome. The boy from Edinburgh rose majestically to thunder through the Spanish rearguard in a fashion modern-day Catalan hero Carles Puyol would have been proud of and directed a perfect header with power and precision past the bewildered home goalkeeper. Clark wheeled to the right, both arms held aloft in salute to the diehard United fans who had made the trip, and in that moment must have known that he would forever be part of Dundee United. High above him, the giant electronic scoreboard read Barcelona 1 Dundee United 1. It gave United a 2-1 aggregate lead and the semi-finals beckoned.

> "When a defining moment comes along, you can...define the moment or let the moment define you."
>
> **Kevin Costner, actor, in the film *Tin Cup***

When Iain Ferguson's header made it 2-1 on the night and 3-1 on aggregate the mission was completed and the McLean bandwagon rolled merrily towards another landmark in the proud history of Dundee United Football Club. With the superstars of Barcelona despatched, Gary Lineker included, there were no teams left in the competition to hold any fears for the determined and well-drilled Tangerines.

While the win in Catalonia did not bring with it a trophy, it meant far more to the legions of United supporters in fact. What it did was prove that their club was no longer a purely Scottish entity, they had a side that could go out into Europe and fly the

Arabs flag with distinction. Yes there had been domestic success beyond the wildest dreams of a set of supporters who in the not too dim and distant past had been watching Second Division football, but until then the European experiences had been bittersweet.

The unbridled joy of a 2-0 victory against Italian cracks Roma in 1984/85 had been tempered by the pain of the 3-0 reverse in the return leg in Rome. The highly credible 2-2 draw against Manchester United at Old Trafford in 1985/86 was countered by the agony of the 3-2 defeat at Tannadice, which left McLean wondering what he had to do to take his team to the next stage on the biggest stage of all.

That night in Barcelona it all came together. It was not only the right result on the night, but one that brought the correct outcome in the two-legged tie. United put one of football's most famous names to the sword but also won themselves a place in the hat for the next round. The team's reputation was enhanced immeasurably with two nods of the head from Clark and Ferguson.

It began to appear as though a place in the final was written in the stars and nothing would get in the way. Borussia Monchengladbach found that to their cost in the last four of the UEFA Cup when Iain Ferguson and Ian Redford scored in the second leg, after a goalless first tie in Dundee, without reply by the Germans. All of a sudden United stood on the brink of joining Celtic, Rangers and Aberdeen on Scotland's roll of honour as European winners.

The team standing between them and that achievement were IFK Gothenburg. The Swedes were talented and technically able, but confidence was brimming after the earlier exploits by the Tannadice troops. A 1-0 defeat in Sweden in the opening game of the two-legged affair failed to dent that belief and for the first time ever a Scottish club had the chance to claim one of the continent's big prizes on home soil.

Tannadice was packed to the rafters on 20 May 1987 as more than 20,000 Arabs sought to see their heroes lift the trophy. The side entrusted with that task had Billy Thomson in goal behind John Holt, Maurice Malpas, David Narey, John Clark, Jim McInally, Iain Ferguson, Kevin Gallacher, Billy Kirkwood, Paul Sturrock and Ian Redford. Eamon Bannon and Paul Hegarty made cameos from the bench on that fateful day.

Unfortunately, the Swedes had not read the script and contrived to rob the home side of their moment of glory, lifting the distinctive UEFA Cup at the end of a hard-fought 1-1 draw that gave them a 2-1 win on aggregate. The Scandinavians had gone into the lead just twenty-two minutes into the match when Lennart Nilsson hammered a low shot past Thomson from inside the box.

A Dundee United equaliser at least gave a glimmer of hope – and when it came the goal was once again from Clark, who was proving adept at rising to the big occasion. This time it was not from his head but from the outside of his left boot after a twisting turn on the edge of the IFK box which a striker half his height would have been proud of. He had neatly collected the ball on the D of the penalty area, and swivelled on his right foot before sending a delightful shot arcing away from the outstretched arm of the despairing goalkeeper and into the top left corner of the net. It was a beautiful piece of play and proved that he had a wonderful touch when necessary.

Clark's classy goal, despite proving fruitless at the end of the ninety minutes, hinted at his beginnings in the game. While remembered as a brute of a defender, he started as a forward and had the ability on the deck to go with that role. It ensured he could be pushed forward as an ancillary striker when required and in the closing stages of that UEFA Cup final, his promptings in and around the opposition penalty area almost won a way back into the match. Ultimately it was not to be, but the final destination in the line for runners-up medals was only part of the story for the desperately unlucky Arabs team. The incredible journey was just as important and for the versatile young player, who was just twenty-two when the final tie was played, it was a passage in his life that would never be forgotten. Even in the modern era of Champions League football and the seemingly never-ending trail of glamour games, few British players can claim to have played at the Nou Camp and won. It is an even more select band who can say they have scored on that most romantic of football stages – and John Clark will always be one of that elite crew. He remains the last Scot to have scored for a Scottish club in a European final to give him his own small slice of trivia.

He is also one of the few men in modern football to have turned his back on the professional game on a point of principle – and part of an even smaller band to have had the guts to stand up to Jim McLean at the same time. Despite enjoying success from a young age, Clark stunned Dundee United fans when he announced he was quitting life as a footballer to go to sea as a trawlerman on his father's boat.

When he went to inform Jim McLean of his decision he expected an attempt to talk him out of his shock move. Instead he was told to pack his bags and head for the ocean wave, not before McLean thanked him for his efforts and wished him well in his new career. As it happened life at sea was not enough to keep Clark away from the game he loved, with a return to United following his dalliance with the new job. Landing prawns at Port Seton, round the coast from his native Edinburgh, transpired not to be as much fun as scoring goals in major European ties. He spent those few weeks away from Tannadice clearing his head and steeling himself for another crack at life as one of McLean's gang. When he made the call to tell his former manager he wanted a reprieve, he was labelled a 'stupid bugger' by his one-time mentor. Still, McLean did take him back in an instant and toyed with giving him an immediate first-team return against Rangers despite his lack of training or match practice. In the end he had to settle for a more sedate reintroduction, in a reserve match against the Ibrox side, but was still welcomed back into the fold and his decision to stand up to McLean and walk away actually proved to be a brave rather than foolish act as his relationship with the boss strengthened on the back of his defiance.

He wasn't the first Scottish player to turn his back on football for a career in the fishing industry. Way back in the 1950s, Aberdeen lost star striker Harry Yorston when he quit in his prime to take up a position as a porter at the Granite City's fish market. Unlike Yorston, Clark had a change of heart and won a second crack at his first love. Mind you, Yorston did have his own slice of good fortune when, in later life, he struck the pools jackpot to supplement the fish-market wage which in those days was more lucrative than that of a top-class footballer.

Clark quickly realised that he would only get one shot at football and reversed his decision early enough to play on, not returning for financial gain but for the love of the game and of the club that he had been with since his teenage days. Before making his first-team debut in 1982 he had spent several character-building campaigns in the reserve side and was a prolific scorer for the second string, well equipped to dealing with the man's world of senior football even as a youngster.

Clark's physical presence made him a player who stood out from the crowd. Throughout his time at Tannadice he faced a constant battle to keep his weight in check, with regular stints on the scales orchestrated by his manager in an attempt to persuade him to shed excess pounds. Sometimes it worked, sometimes it didn't – but Clark was a player who could get away with it, putting his bulk to good use with his dominant displays and thunderous shots. Standing 6ft tall, his weight rose from 14st during his prime years to 17st by the time he was plying his trade away from Tannadice with Falkirk. While turning out for Gala Fairydean as player-manager there was an extra stone on top of that figure, yet he continued to pose a threat in the opposition box thanks to his years of experience.

Clark's appeal to the supporters had much to do with his physique. He had the stature to put the fear of death into the opposition, whether playing up front or at the back, and his mere presence gave peace of mind. Like the burly bouncer on the pub door, it was a not-so-gentle reminder that this team was not one to be messed with. The other benefit to his physical attributes was the simple power to weight ratio that provided a shot like a cannon, a weapon used to great effect time and time again until his time in tangerine had run its course.

Clark, tied to United on one of McLean's infamous long-term contracts for the bulk of his career, broke free in 1994 when Stoke City manager Joe Jordan came calling and succeeded with a £150,000 bid. That was in February, just twelve weeks before the United team-mates he left behind collected the Scottish Cup at Hampden. It was a cruel blow for a player who deserved to share in that success. Instead of the highs of the national stadium, Clark was sampling the lows of life in England. Jordan was dismissed early in his first full season with the Potters and Clark followed him out of the exit door, desperate to escape from a miserable period with the Second Division outfit, having had little chance to woo the Stoke supporters in the way he had won the overwhelming support of the Tannadice faithful. The English itch had been scratched and it was time to return to base.

Jim Jefferies, a man who over the course of time has proved his talent as an astute judge of a player, was in charge of Falkirk at that time and was one of the versatile star's admirers. Jefferies paid £100,000 to take Clark back to the Premier Division in September 1994 as he added experience to his plucky team. The former United man's proven versatility at the top level was a big draw for teams who courted Clark, although the Bairns signed him primarily as a striker as they attempted to return him to his roots. He had not been appreciated by fans south of the border, but Scottish crowds up and down the land knew exactly what he would bring to the table.

The Big Man had started life at Tannadice as a forward, becoming one of a string of players converted from an attacking role to take a defensive berth under McLean. Just as Paul Hegarty, Tom McAdam and Jackie Copland had to drop back through the side to thrive, there was a similar conversion for Clark. Jim McLean had mused that it would have been more beneficial to have been able to turn defenders into devastating attackers, but in truth he was glad to have a dependable new stopper to call upon as his tried and trusted team entered a period of change. The transition began to take shape in the winter of 1986, when Clark was utilised as a centre half against Universitaea Craiova in the UEFA Cup.

Mind you, Clark proved he still knew the way to goal when he netted with a header in a 3-0 victory. It proved to be the beginning of a lengthy tour of defensive duty.

Clark settled into life as a centre half with ease, covering the ground with a pace that made a mockery of the concerns about his bulk. For a spell he was also put to use as a right back, where his attacking instincts were able to flourish and his fearsome tackling struck terror into the hearts of wingers throughout the land. With a neat line in crunching challenges and his legendary pile-drivers in his armoury there was seldom a dull moment. There is no doubt Clark could divide opinion, but he became a hero to chunks of the Tannadice crowd with his unorthodox style and sheer brute force. In 2010 that contribution was recognised when he was welcomed to the Dundee United hall of fame. It was a fitting way to mark his long and committed service to the cause. The elevation of Clark to hall of fame status was warmly received on the night and when he was invited back to Tannadice in 2007 to take a bow when United tackled Barcelona during the Spanish side's training trip to the east coast there was a similarly nostalgic reaction.

The fondness for Clark, a modest and bashful former player who never craved media attention or the trappings of his sporting celebrity, is linked to the warmth for the period in which he played. He made his debut as an eighteen-year-old substitute against Viking Stavanger in the 1982/83 UEFA Cup and also featured against St Mirren in the Scottish Cup that term, as well as making his first start for the club in a league match against the Buddies at Tannadice during the triumphant charge towards the Premier Division title. With that one starting appearance and one further appearance from the bench in the league, Clark did not earn a medal and when the badges did follow they were silver rather than gold. Clark had to settle for runners-up medals following the League Cup final of 1984/85 and the Scottish Cup showdowns in 1987, 1988 and 1991. He arrived just too late for the league win in 1983 and left just too soon to play a part in the 1994 Scottish Cup win, enduring heartbreak at every turn in between despite so many high spots and big game experiences. Clark could be considered one of the unluckiest players on the United rollcall but for the fact that he sampled moments that many others before and after him could not even dream of getting close to.

His last playing involvement on the hallowed turf was as a Dunfermline player in the mid-1990s. After returning to Scotland with Falkirk in 1994, Clark spent just three months at Brockville before moving on to the Pars. He spent half a season with the Fife side before a second brief stint with Falkirk during the 1996/97 campaign. During that term he also made a one-game cameo appearance for Ross County, helping out old team-mate Neale Cooper during his tenure in charge of the Highlanders, before winding down with Berwick Rangers prior to his appointment as manager of Gala Fairydean in 2001. Like so many of Jim McLean's former protégés, Clark took to the coaching game like a duck to water. He led the non-league borderers to the final of the King's Cup and into the Scottish Cup, where they dumped senior opponents Stirling Albion out of the competition before bowing out against Forfar Athletic. Clark was tempted to Whitehill Welfare within two years and again had success, helping the club stave off the threat of relegation and then leading them to the Qualifying Cup before parting company with the East of Scotland League outfit and stepping back from the semi-professional game. With the tag of coach surrendered, Clark is free to revel in the role of

Arabs hero once more. More than twenty years on he could be forgiven for allowing himself a daydream now and again and a flashback to the scoreboard shining in the Spanish night sky: Barcelona 1 Dundee United 1. The goal that changed his life forever.

1986-1998
DAVE BOWMAN

Magic Moment: The 1995/96 season dawned and Bowman's service was recognised with two honours – a testimonial and, more importantly, the coveted club captaincy.

Tangerines Career: Games 428. Goals 12. Caps 6.

IF EVER there was a man of contradictions it must surely be Dave Bowman. Known the length and breadth of the country by his football nickname of 'Psycho', he was the fair-haired destroyer who put the steely core into Dundee United in the 1980s and 1990s. He was the player famously red-carded five times in one match as a veteran playing for Forfar and hit with a seventeen-match ban as a result. Yet Bowman is also a man who thought nothing of turning to floristry for a career outside of football, a man who is now charged with being the face of Dundee United in the community and a man who has passionately taken on the role as charity fundraiser for a cause dedicated to the memory of two late Tannadice supporters. He is a legend and cult hero rolled into one intriguing package.

> "I've had teams with enforcers. I've had teams with no enforcers. I've won with both. The reality is you need an enforcer, in my book, if he can play the game."
>
> **Guy Boucher, ice hockey coach**

The Bowman story is one best told by starting at the end of his playing career. While he was no stranger to the referee's notebook as a United player, nothing could prepare him for the bureaucracy gone mad that awaited him during the twilight of his career with Forfar Athletic. He was thirty-seven years old and playing football for love, not money, in the Second Division for the Angus outfit. When he took umbrage at team-mate Robbie Horn's dismissal during a game at Stranraer, the referee took a dislike to the tone of his protests and sent him off. A further four red cards followed as Bowman continued the debate on his way off the park. Having been shown four red cards the previous season, during a defeat against Berwick and banned for seven matches on that occasion he was braced for what was likely to follow. The seventeen-match suspension took it to a whole new level, making Bowman officially Scottish football's baddest bad boy of all time.

He may not have had that tag whilst on the books at Tannadice but he had a reputation as a fierce competitor and it was his rugged approach to the game that won him so many admirers among Arabs. He gave his all for the tangerine and black cause every time he pulled on the jersey and gave teeth to a succession of United teams during good times and bad.

If you fancy finding out just how tough an opponent Bowman is, you still can. Simply pull together a minimum donation of £100 to United's nominated skin cancer charity and your team, whether five-a-side, seven-a-side or eleven-a-side, can take on Bowman and his group of former United stars. Running that charity challenge scheme is just one of many strings to the Tannadice legend's bow, enlisting the help of former team-mates such as Ray McKinnon, Gary Bollan, Grant Johnson, Darren Jackson and

Paddy Connelly for the friendly contests. The choice of skin cancer as the chosen cause relates to the deaths of young United supporters Alan Clarke and Ally Watt, both lost to the condition in recent years.

Playing is now simply about having fun, but the veteran midfielder will never lose the competitive edge that made him a snarling force to be reckoned with throughout the 1980s and 1990s.

Bowman told me: 'The response to the charity matches has been really good. At one stage we had more games on the fixture list than the first team and the hard thing is being able to get everyone to commit to all of the dates that we would like to play, but everyone finds the time. The good thing is we all still love playing the game, especially when it's for such a good cause. We have managed to raise a few thousand pounds already and there is still plenty of interest. It is all laughs and jokes – until we get on the park, then it gets really competitive. Darren Jackson laughs at me, telling me it's only a charity game while I'm going bananas at the referee. Old habits die hard.'

That spirit ensured brushes with the Hampden beaks started at a young age, with the fresh-faced Bowman seeing red for the first time when he was a seventeen-year-old making his way in the game with Hearts. The former Parsons Green School pupil, who played his boys' club football with respected capital outfit Salveson, spent four years at Tynecastle before being tempted south, to the country of his birth, for a spell with Coventry City in the closing weeks of 1984. Two years later he was back in Scotland, the country of his heart and the one he represented on the international stage, with Dundee United and the twelve-year love affair with the Tannadice faithful began. Bowman, born in

Tunbridge Wells but brought up in Edinburgh, spent long enough on Tayside to be awarded a testimonial against city rivals Dundee and it was no surprise that the Arabs turned out in force to show their appreciation for one of their favourite sons.

Bowman arrived in May 1986 alongside midfield sidekick Jim McInally in a deal worth £130,000 to selling club Coventry City. It proved to be some of the best money ever spent by McLean, who grabbed himself a bargain with a pair of wily characters who belied their tender years to add real bite to the Arabs squad.

Bowman, who had been capped at under-21 level by Scotland, was just twenty-two and had eighteen months experience of English football under his belt. He had been parachuted into a Coventry squad toiling at the wrong end of the First Division table, embroiled in the perennial fight for survival, signed by Bobby Gould but quickly falling under the auspices of Scottish coach Don Mackay when he took over from Gould in December 1984. Bowman played his part in keeping Coventry in the top flight but before long was back on more familiar tracks.

He had frequently been linked with a switch to United and the lengthy pursuit paid off. The double deal for McInally and Bowman was funded by the sale of Billy Kirkwood and Stuart Beedie to Hibs; in exchange they bagged a player in Bowman who had cost Coventry £150,000 when he joined them from Hearts eighteen months previously. McInally, who had been sent to play for Dundee on loan during his days as a youngster at Celtic, had wracked up fees of £110,000 across his transfers from Parkhead to Nottingham Forest and then on to Coventry. He too was just twenty-two and was a player who had the potential to earn his way several times over. Beedie, who had been a bit-part player, and Kirkwood, a valuable squad man who was looking towards his thirtieth birthday, had served their time and it was time for the next generation to make their mark.

Bowman and McInally arrived at a club who had finished third in the Premier Division and reached the last four of the Scottish Cup. The signs all pointed to further success, on the back of the glory days of the early 1980s, and the debut season proved to be a wonderful education in just what being a Dundee United player was all about. Bowman was by no means an automatic selection in that first term but did appear in twenty-nine of the forty-four league fixtures, coming from the bench in ten of those, as McLean's evolving side pushed the Old Firm all the way. They had to be content with third place, behind champions Rangers and runners-up Celtic, but of course it was European football that dominated life on Tayside that season. The young midfielder played in the early ties against RC Lens and Universitaea Craiova before dropping out for the middle section of the UEFA Cup run. He returned to the fray just in time for the vital semi-final second leg against Borussia Mönchengladbach, when goals from Iain Ferguson and Ian Redford sealed United's passage to the final after a goalless first leg at Tannadice.

Bowman also played in the first leg of the final against IFK Gothenburg in Sweden but after that 1-0 reverse he missed out on a place in the side for the climax at Tannadice, handing his No.8 shirt to Kevin Gallacher following his promotion from the bench.

In between the two Gothenburg contests, Bowman had sampled his first Scottish Cup final, turning out in the 1-0 extra-time defeat against St Mirren at Hampden. It was a painful introduction to the harsh realties of cup final football, but his time would come.

He was also a member of the defeated side in the 1988 Scottish Cup final against Celtic and a goal scorer in the 4-3 loss against Motherwell in the 1991 showpiece game. He could at least console himself with the man of the match award on the back of a typically industrious display in the extra-time nerve shredder.

The tears turned to cheers in 1994 when he ran out at Hampden as a key man for Ivan Golac's Scottish Cup-winning side, by which time a player who was once among the young upstarts under McLean had become one of the wise old owls of the continental manager's side.

Throughout the eight years between his arrival and that crowning glory on the turf of the national stadium, the star had been a driving force for his team. His energetic performances were coupled with legendary defensive resolve and confidence in possession. His personality also shone through and Bowman became a popular figure in the United dressing room, able to lift spirits with his boundless enthusiasm.

The tag the fans gave him tells its own story, as Bowman recalls:

'The Psycho nickname was one the supporters came up with. At one point they even had t-shirts with the shower scene from the film printed on them. To me, football is like every other sport – if you're going to take part, you do it to win. I'm exactly the same if I'm playing golf, I don't play just for the sake of going round a nice course. I work with the Dundee United youth teams, from under-13 through to under-19, and that will to win is the one thing you simply cannot teach. You can teach many things and create lots of good habits, but that isn't one of them.

'Of course the other good habits are important too. If you look at Ryan Giggs, he'll track back to try and block a cross in the last minute of a game that his side are winning 2-0. He does that because it has been drummed into him and he would be the same whether he was earning £100 a week or £100,000 a week. We try and instil those same things in our young players. It is important to get the small things right.'

Bowman's endeavours with Dundee United were recognised by the Scotland management team in March 1992 when he was called up to the full international squad for the first time in his career. It came as a bolt from the tangerine to the Tartan Army, but for national team boss Andy Roxburgh it was a logical move.

Roxburgh had last managed Bowman when he was in charge of the Scotland under-18 side that stormed to victory in the youth European Championships in Helsinki in 1982. It remains the country's only international tournament victory. Along with contemporaries Paul McStay and Dave McPherson he helped Scotland to the quarter-finals of the youth World Cup in Mexico the following year.

The coach watched from a distance as his young protégé matured as a player and had no qualms about pulling him up to the top level.

Roxburgh said: 'He is very adaptable and an excellent team player. We have been lacking a midfield powerhouse recently and David fits the bill. Since Murdo MacLeod and Roy Aitken drifted away from the scene we haven't had many players in the ball-winning category. I spoke to his manager, Jim McLean, last night and he more than endorses our decision.'

McLean was not a man predisposed towards praising his players. Yet he had an understandable soft spot for Bowman, one of the few players in football who never failed to deliver 100 per cent effort. McLean greeted the call-up by saying: 'If anyone deserves the honour it's Dave Bowman, who gets ten out of ten from me every time he goes out on the park.' It was high praise indeed from the highest Tannadice office.

He was twenty-eight years old when he joined the pool for a friendly against Finland at Hampden, joined by fellow rookie Gordon Marshall. The duo had been classmates at school in Edinburgh and remained close friends, with Bowman serving as Marshall's best man in later life. It was a neat twist of fate that brought the two of them into the international reckoning at the same time as Roxburgh tried to find the formula to invigorate his side.

Only one of the old pals got to play against the Finns and it was the United man. Bowman was given the full ninety minutes to prove himself as an international midfielder and did himself no harm at all with his display in a 1-1 draw, with midfield partner Paul McStay scoring the goal for the home side. He was taken on tour with Roxburgh's side two months later and featured again in a 1-0 friendly win against the United States in Denver as a substitute. It was 1993 when Bowman got his second start for Scotland, again in a challenge match, at the heart of the midfield against Germany at Ibrox. It was the game in which former Tannadice team-mate Duncan Ferguson rattled the woodwork with a dramatic overhead kick, but it was the visitors who emerged with a 1-0 victory.

It gave the Arabs favourite a friendly record of won one, drawn one and lost one. His scorecard in competitive internationals was exactly the same, with Bowman part featuring in three World Cup qualifiers in 1993 to complete his cap collection and take his total appearances to six.

His first World Cup tie was against Estonia in Tallinn when goals from Kevin Gallacher, John Collins and Scott Booth gave

Roxburgh's men a 3-0 win. Bowman was again alongside McStay in the engine room, proving well suited to the game at the highest level.

He then helped Scotland to a 1-1 draw against Switzerland at Pittodrie, a game in which Collins was again on target, before earning a crack at the biggest game of his time with the national squad: Italy in Rome. It was a match played in front of 61,000 passionate supporters, an attendance boosted by the large Tartan Army contingent. Despite Kevin Gallacher's seventeenth-minute goal, it ended in a 3-1 defeat and also signalled Bowman's swansong as Roxburgh turned to fresh blood. It was another Tannadice product, Billy McKinlay, who was drafted in for the next World Cup qualifier in Malta. The half-dozen internationals came as a bonus for Bowman, who looked to have missed the Scotland boat before his late call-up by Roxburgh. He was not the most high-profile player in the national set-up but he had the confidence to live in any football company and those who had played against him on domestic duty knew exactly the qualities he would bring to the table.

He was the type of character every player wanted beside them in the trenches when the going got tough. Maurice Malpas, David Hannah and Bowman were the three men Ivan Golac and Billy Kirkwood called upon more than any others during the struggle to beat relegation in the 1994/95 campaign. Even the efforts of those three could not prevent the fall from grace but Kirkwood regrouped his men and led them to promotion from the First Division at the first attempt the following term.

While the 1995/96 campaign brought the joy of earning a return to the top flight, it also brought pain for the midfield general. In the autumn of 1995 his strength of character was tested to the full when he suffered a sickening injury, shattering a cheekbone and spending three months on the sidelines after surgery to rebuild the damaged portion of his face. He was fitted with a protective face mask to help ease him back into competitive football at reserve level. True to form he quickly discarded the protection and was deemed ready for first-team action. Not for Bowman a gentle reintroduction after the shocking injury – instead he was pitched in against the Beastie Boys of Airdrie in a bruising 2-2 draw as a substitute in a pulsating match that had seen his side reduced to nine men before his introduction. Within seconds, he was back in the thick of the action and giving as good as he got without a thought to the fragile facial repair that had kept him out for three months.

Bowman was rewarded with a testimonial in August 1995 and he chose the opposition well. No half-hearted friendly for Psycho, instead a city derby against Dundee. The big fear was that he would be suspended for his own big night, having been suspended for four matches at the end of the 1994/95 season. He had to get special dispensation from the SFA to feature in the match.

Bowman, who rose to become captain of United in the 1990s, went on to add a bizarre new chapter to his disciplinary book when he was given his marching orders just three minutes into a showdown with Hibs at Tannadice in 1996. The ordering-off was the result of a tussle with Keith Wright and led to yet another appearance in front of the SFA paragons of virtue. That latest brush with the officials did not stall his club career and he remained an important member of the squad even as the years rolled by and the twilight of his career loomed. Both Kirkwood and his successor Tommy McLean used Bowman's experience to bolster their side, although it was McLean who sanctioned his departure in 1998 as he reshaped his squad on the back of a disappointing seventh-place finish in the league. As it happened, he could have done with Bowman's never-say-die spirit as his team struggled the following season.

After leaving Tannadice in 1998 he spent a season with Raith Rovers, during which time his ability to attract controversy manifested itself when he was involved in a bust-up with the Kirkcaldy side's supporters following an on-field altercation with Raith keeper and former United team-mate Guido Van de Kamp.

An eye-opening year with Hong Kong team Yee Hope, a side bedecked in familiar tangerine and black colours, followed the Rovers' experience. While his troubles in Fife had been on the pitch, on foreign soil it was the human rights issues which pricked at Bowman's conscience. The golf driving range he and his western team-mates would while away their free time on also doubled as a firing range for the executions carried out on a monthly basis. It put brushes with the SFA's disciplinary committee into stark perspective.

After a year with Yee Hope, Bowman returned to base and settled again in Dundee. He was appointed captain of Forfar as he played out his days with the same passion which had made him such a success during his peak years. His seventeen-match ban, by the time the Scottish winter's postponements had been factored in, kept the United favourite sidelined for the best part of six months. Although he returned in time for the end of the 2001/02 season, it proved to be his swansong as a senior player and he bowed out of the professional game after more than twenty years at the sharp end.

It was during his part-time days that he turned to the world of flowers, helping at his father-in-law's floristry business.

By then he was already involved in coaching youngsters at Tannadice and through various managerial changes and restructurings he has retained a key involvement in that area. Bowman is a player ingrained in the past and also with a firm part to play in its future. His current role is heading up United's community schools programme, established in 2008 to help the Arabs reach out to the next generation. Bowman and his team of coaches deliver coaching modules to schools throughout the club's catchment area with an emphasis on combining football with positive social messages. Thousands of children have fallen under the wing of Bowman and his crew and, with support from the Scottish government, there are great hopes that it will be expanded in the years ahead.

Explaining the programme, he said: 'What we offer through the schools is not only good for the pupils but also for us as a club on a few different levels. For one thing it is an opportunity for our young players to get out and try something different by coming out to the schools with us and passing on their skills. It may persuade one or two of them to consider coaching as a career or to look at the potential to study at university for qualifications in that area. The reality is that only two or three per cent of youth team players will go on and progress to the top level, so it does no harm to have an idea of the alternatives out there.

'The main aim is to encourage all of the children to be active. If we can excite them about football and about Dundee United then even better, particularly if they can be encouraged to support the club in the long term. In Dundee we have two teams drawing on the same audience, so it's important to be proactive and give youngsters a genuine feel and affection for Dundee United. By our involvement we're taking the club out into the community.

'I thought we might get twenty or thirty kids enlisted at any one school, but I've seen us have 160 or 170. It has been incredible. It isn't something we make money from. All of the children get a kit, which they wear for all of the sessions for the duration of the eight weeks we are at their school, as well as match tickets. Hopefully they also take a lot from the coaching sessions we put on. The flip side for us is that we also get an opportunity to spend an extended period of time with each group, so if there is a young player who stands out we can see them at close quarters. Already a few gems have been found that way.'

While Bowman is dedicated to his part in nurturing prospective young players and supporters, he has not forgotten the past. He has taken it upon himself to form the Dundee United Former Players Association and is in the early stages of pulling together a database of former players to build links between the old boys and the club. Every former player is entitled to two tickets for every home game under the constitution of the club and Bowman is relishing the opportunity to bring familiar faces back together at Tannadice, and back to a city which has become a home from home for the capital city boy.

He said: 'I remember when I first joined the club as a player, Paul Hegarty, who is from Edinburgh too, said he would never move back there. I thought to myself "that'll be right" – but twenty-five years on, we're both still here. It's a great part of the country to stay and there have been a lot of people who have always come back, wherever their career has taken them. Jocky Scott, with all of the places he has worked, is the perfect example. I couldn't have predicted the length of time I would spend at the club, but I was fortunate that the Dundee United supporters were great with me. I had a wonderful relationship with the crowd and that makes the bond with a club that much stronger. I used to get people coming up to me saying, "You used to be my dad's favourite player." Now I'm getting people saying, "You used to be my grandad's favourite player!"'

A player who gave everything for the club as a player is now putting just as much back into the club in his plethora of new roles, each one being attacked with the same passion and vigour that made him a hero in the first place.

1987-1992

MIXU PAATELAINEN

Magic Moment: The young Finnish rookie introduced himself to Scottish football with a debut goal against St Mirren in 1987. Big Mixu had arrived.

Tangerines Career: Games 173. Goals 47. Caps 70 (Finland).

TO BECOME a cult hero at one club could be the result of a stroke of luck or outrageous fortune. To become a cult hero at five different clubs is no coincidence and that is exactly what Paatelainen went out and did in both England and Scotland. After being taken to heart by the Tannadice fans, his first football love, he went on to win over the Aberdeen support with the same rumbustious approach to the game that bowled over the Arabs faithful when he was unleashed on an unsuspecting Scottish football public in the late 1980s.

"Weak men wait for opportunities, strong men make them."

Orison Marden, author

At Bolton, his third club during an exhilarating tour of British football, he became a player who remains part of club folklore and when he moved to Hibs he produced bursts of goals which could not fail to get the Easter Road faithful on his side. At Cowdenbeath, in his first managerial position, he achieved the same rapport and an everlasting place in the club's list of heroes.

Paatelainen has been loved and cherished wherever he has gone, and attitude has to be a major part of the attraction to the tens of thousands of supporters who roared him on. Nothing was done in half measures with the Finn around and his fearless displays made him an obvious target for the affection of paying customers who expected their troops to go the extra mile for the team. He was a forward who gave the impression he would run through a barn door to score a goal – and if there was no door available, an opposition defender was the next best thing.

It is Dundee United who can take the credit for unearthing the rough diamond with a serious cutting edge. He signed for the Terrors at the end of October 1987, initially joining on a part-time contract having impressed during a trial period with the squad. The club had first been alerted by a contact of his father, who had business connections in Scotland. Up to that point the twenty-year-old had been playing his football for Haka Valkeakoski in his home town, as well as the Finland under-21 and Olympic teams. He had come up through the ranks, first playing Third Division football in Finland as a raw and ambitious fifteen-year-old desperate to make it big. He dreamt of one day flying the nest and testing himself in one of Europe's more recognised leagues and trained day in and day out to make it a reality. His inspiration was his father Matti, a fifty-times capped Finland international, while his fallback position was to pursue a career in medicine and follow in the footsteps of his mother, who is a doctor.

Medicine's loss proved to be football's gain as Jim McLean concluded the deal that set Paatelainen on the path to a long and prosperous career as a sportsman. His international ambitions were not harmed by his move to British football and he quickly amassed a haul of Finland caps. With thirty-eight appearances to his credit, his time with the Finns came to a shuddering halt when he chose to play for Aberdeen ahead of his country on one occasion in 1994. Manager Tommy Lindholm took grave offence, but the hatchet was eventually buried and he went on to play seventy times for his country and eventually earned the captaincy. That was the honour he had strived for from the time he started kicking a ball in his home village and, as he had confidently predicted, he went on to achieve it through a combination of natural ability and good old-fashioned hard work.

After agreeing to United's offer, he went straight into the squad to face St Mirren at Tannadice on 31 October 1987 when Kevin Gallacher, Paul Sturrock and Ian Redford had all been ruled out of the match due to injury. When he signed Paatelainen, Jim McLean said: 'We are expecting a lot of the lad. Playing him tomorrow may appear to be a bit of a gamble, but injuries have forced our hand. I am confident, however, that he will do really well.'

United fell to a 3-2 defeat but there was a personal triumph for the twenty-year-old rookie, who marked his debut with a goal. The unflappable Finn remained in the team as the season wore on, scoring nine goals in nineteen league games which included one in a 2-0 derby win against Dundee and all four in a 4-0 victory against Morton at Cappielow.

He had arrived just in time for the Scottish Cup run that took his new team all the way to the Hampden final against Celtic and had a big role to play in that campaign. As well as being on target in the first-round trouncing of Arbroath, when the Gayfield men were beaten 7-0, he also scored in the semi-final replay against Aberdeen as the nail-biting 1-1 extra-time draw brought about a second replay. Iain Ferguson scored to put the Arabs through but there was heartache for Paatelainen in his first taste of the cup final experience as the Hoops came back from a goal down to win 2-1. Paatelainen had trooped off the park with twenty minutes to play, replaced by John Clark, when the score was still 1-0 in United's favour. He could only watch helplessly from the sidelines as his team-mates let the match slip away from them.

The youngster had proved himself as a talented Premier Division performer, adjusting quickly to the pace of the Scottish game and demonstrating the physicality that defenders loathed and the Tannadice supporters loved. Duncan Shearer, a former team-mate of the Finn's at Aberdeen, has described his stature as akin to that of great redwood tree and few would disagree with that assessment.

It was Paatelainen's strength and determination that made him such a favourite at every club he played for through a distinguished playing career on both sides of the border. As well as muscle, he had brain, with composure well ahead of his modest years. Pressure was not in the Scandinavian's impressive vocabulary, with McLean adopting him as the team's penalty-taker in his first full season as a professional.

With that ability to stay calm in any circumstances, the attacking menace had the temperament to succeed. At 5ft 11in tall and with a powerful frame, he also had the make-up of a perfect centre forward as well as an aggressive streak that made the most of those qualities. With a left foot that packed a considerable punch and aerial ability, there was not a lot that the Finn couldn't do.

In his first season, entering the fray three months into the campaign, he notched nine goals in seventeen starts and two substitute appearances in the league as well as two in seven matches in the Scottish Cup to creep into double figures with eleven goals from twenty-six appearances.

In the 1988/89 season he built on that initial success as he established himself, not just as a force at Tannadice but in Scottish football. He topped the Arabs scoring chart with his return of ten goals in thirty-three league games, four in six Scottish Cup ties and three in three League Cup matches. Although Paatelainen drew a blank in the European Cup Winners' Cup he ended the year with seventeen goals in forty-five appearances across all competitions to finish four ahead of Kevin Gallacher in the race for the golden boot.

The fourth-place finish ensured UEFA Cup football for the following term and it was in that competition that the Finn got off the mark in continental competition, scoring against Royal Antwerp. That goal helped him retain his place as the club's top scorer for the 1989/90 season but in truth it was a difficult season. His nine goals across the league, domestic cups and UEFA Cup were all it took to hold the honour and it pointed to the side's serious problem with scoring goals. In thirty-six Premier Division matches, McLean's team could only muster the same number of goals. It was still enough to finish fourth, but it was a cause of concern for the manager as Paatelainen and Darren Jackson failed to break into double figures.

Jackson took the mantle as the main man into 1990/91, with Paatelainen's appearances mainly from the bench, as Christian Dailly emerged from the youth ranks to establish himself as another option in attack and Duncan Ferguson also began to make an impression with the first team. It was a similar story the following year as the Finn had to content himself with a staccato contribution to the cause, with every starting appearance matched by one from the bench throughout the campaign. By then it was Ferguson who was leading the line and providing the bite to the

United forward line and the writing was on the wall for the popular Scandinavian. He was still wanted at Tannadice, but remaining would have meant settling for a support role and that was never likely to meet with his ambitions.

He was rough and rugged and the type of player who would never fade into the background. It was little surprise that other teams had sat up and taken notice of his struggles to win a place in the Arabs team – and even less of a surprise that it was one of the defenders that Mika-Matti, to give Mixu his Sunday name, terrorised that stepped in to sign him when McLean decided to cash in his chips on a player who had cost him nothing to sign.

It was Scotland and Aberdeen legend Willie Miller who lured Paatelainen away from Tannadice with the promise of a bumper contract at Pittodrie. It cost him £400,000 to make his first signing as Tangerines boss – but he was confident it would be money well spent as he sent out a signal that he meant business. No player in the Premier Divison displayed that up-and-at-them spirit of Paatelainen. His versatility, with the ability to play wide left or through the middle, made him a valuable squad member.

McLean had been keen to keep the big Finn on Tayside but when the offer of a new Arabs contract was rejected there was little option but to sell to the highest bidder.

The Pittodrie crowd were thrilled with their acquisition, although his time in the Granite City was short and sweet. In 1994 Paatelainen's performances drew a long line of English talent spotters north. Joe Jordan at Stoke City and Mick McCarthy at Millwall were both keen – but it was Bruce Rioch at Bolton who won the race. He paid £300,000 to take the forward south. In his first season he scored twenty goals in thirty-eight matches for the Dons, although he struggled to hold down a permanent place in his second term. The move to England put the spark back into Paatelainen's game, with a last-gasp bid by Hearts to keep him in the north failing.

His time at Burnden Park was a success, with Paatelainen's goal against Swindon in the League Cup semi-final helping the Lancashire side through to a final showdown with Liverpool in 1995. He was also part of the squad that won the First Division championship in 1997 to take the team into the top flight.

Just weeks after Bolton were defeated 2-1 in the final, Dundee United manager Billy Kirkwood failed in an ambitious bid to take the striker back to Tannadice. Kirkwood had a £500,000 offer sanctioned by the board, desperate to bounce back to the Premier Division at the first attempt, but was told by the Trotters that he was not for sale.

It would have been hugely unpopular to sell a big man who had become a big favourite. Surely you know you have achieved cult status when you get a name check in one of the country's best-loved comedy series. That honour was bestowed upon Paatelainen when his distinctive moniker popped up in Peter Kay's hugely popular *Phoenix Nights*, the show set in Bolton. When bouncers Max and Paddy made a hoax call to club owner Brian Potter, they chose Mixu Paatelainen as the name for a phantom caller from the coroner's office. It might have been lost on large swathes of the population, but in several corners of the country the fleeting reference was guaranteed to raise a laugh.

Paatelainen's reach was extended to the English midlands when, at the end of his Bolton contract in 1997, the Helsinki-born hitman moved on to Wolves under Mark McGhee.

He returned to the Scottish game with Hibs in 1998, the first of two spells at Easter Road sandwiching a period in France with

Strasbourg during the 2001/02 season. After Hibs he wound up at St Johnstone in 2003 and then St Mirren the following year. He began to cut his coaching teeth with the Hibs youth teams and moved on to work with the first-team squads at both St Johnstone and St Mirren as old father time got to grips with his own playing career.

Having worked at a high level, he dropped right to the foot of the Scottish football pyramid to take on his first managerial challenge. Cowdenbeath, a team that had just missed out on promotion in the 2004/05 campaign, is a club with a proud tradition of unearthing managerial stars of the future and in Paatelainen they struck gold. He had the same ambition in management that had driven him forward as a player and vowed to be firm, disciplined and organised. He had taken tips from the best, including McLean and Bolton boss Bruce Rioch, and was ready to put his own slant on the profession.

The Finn took charge in the summer of 2005 and led the 'Blue Brazil' to the Third Division championship at the first attempt. It was an incredible achievement with a team of perennial strugglers. Just as he had been worshipped as a player, Paatelainen could do no wrong in the eyes of the Central Park fans. His side had played passing football with an attacking bias and thrilled their followers with the title win.

The prize was secured on the last day of the season and flown in by helicopter to mark a fitting end to the club's 125th anniversary season. It was Cowdenbeath's first title win in sixty-seven years and a momentous occasion for the club and the supporters.

The win inspired the book *Helicopter Dreams*, written by lifelong Cowden fan Ron Ferguson. Even after Paatelainen announced his decision to move on, Ferguson was glowing in his praise of the man. He said:

'As both a journalist and a minister, I have had dealings with many people in all walks of life, and it takes a lot to impress a cynical hack. Well, I am impressed by Mixu Paatelainen. You can tell the best football managers not by the statements they make to the press but by the results they produce on the park. Think Jock Stein. The only mistake Stein ever made was to turn down the first and best offer of a manager's job he ever had – the hot seat at Central Park. But he had the gift of getting the best out of players, turning them into heroes filled with self-belief, as at Dunfermline, Easter Road and Parkhead.

'Paatelainen is a natural leader. He has charisma, authority, a sense of purpose, clear goals, and an ability to communicate his ideas to those he works with. He is self-confident without being arrogant. He has a sense of where he is going. It would not at all surprise me if Mixu goes to the very top as a manager. I recognise that this is a foolhardy thing to say in print on the basis of one season in the Scottish Third Division. I'm also aware that just as injuries can cut short a wonderful playing career – just ask Craig Levein – so events can happen in football that derail even the best of coaches. Nevertheless, I will back my hunch about this man.'

During his one-season wonder at Cowdenbeath he was aided and abetted by his brothers, Markus and Mikko, after taking them over from Finland to join the promotion push. Both proved able performers at that level and earned a trial with Aberdeen. Markus went on to play at a higher level with Caley Thistle, although injury curtailed his involvement with the Highlanders.

While the younger Paatelainen siblings were catching the eye with composed performances for the club, it was nothing when compared to the attention being lavished on their big brother. As happened with Craig Levein previously, the Fifers had to be braced for the big guns moving in. While Levein had been tempted from Cowdenbeath to Hearts in 2000, it was little known Finnish outfit TPS Turku who moved in to pinch their boss in October 2006. The club had big funds to throw at a push for a run in European football and viewed the former international as the man to mastermind it. He led them to third place in the league before winding up back in Scotland as manager of Hibs in 2008, stepping into the breach after the departure of John Collins, but struggled to make the type of impact at Easter Road that he hoped for. Paatelainen had a lofty reputation to live up to after his playing days elevated him to heady heights. As with so many returns, it proved not to be a happy one. Two sixth-place finishes in the highly competitive SPL were no disgrace but it was not enough to keep him in the top job. Paatelainen left Leith at the end of the 2008/09 campaign after a muted reaction from the squad to his methods and philosophy, claiming it was time for a change of direction for both parties. He did not reappear until the summer of 2010 when he took charge of Kilmarnock for another crack at SPL management with the Rugby Park side following their narrow escape from relegation under Jimmy Calderwood the previous season. Calderwood had walked away due to the testing circumstances in Ayrshire, with the club heavily indebted and lacking strength in depth. Still, Paatelainen was never one to shirk a challenge as a player and it appears he has retained that determination and stubborn streak in his coaching career.

Kilmarnock had looked at various options for replacing Calderwood, but it was the Finn who rose to the head of their list after a summer spent exhaustively searching for a man tough enough to take on the task of trying to keep the side's valuable top-flight status intact. John Robertson, Czaba Laslo, Alex Rae, and Gus MacPherson were all on the radar but the Rugby Park board found an extra spark in their chosen candidate, the type of appeal that had swayed so many clubs previously. For a coach who from his earliest days at Cowdenbeath preached the necessity for a work ethic and willingness to learn, he would have to bring out the best in a group of players who would have to punch above their weight to survive. It was an ethos that served him so well as a player and which as a manager embroiled in the fight for SPL survival will serve him well in the future.

1991-1992

VICTOR FERREYRA

Magic Moment: A double and some flashes of South American genius on only his second appearance in United colours gave hope that a new shooting star had touched down on Tayside.

Tangerines Career: Games 35. Goals 8. Caps 3 (Argentina).

UNITED HAD enjoyed success with the Scandinavian influx during Jerry Kerr's tenure in the scintillating sixties and then with Kjell Olofsson, Erik Pedersen and Lars Zetterlund in the late nineties. The players from Norway, Sweden and Denmark came with certain guarantees. They were athletic, committed and had a temperament suited to the Scottish game. There were no such guarantees with the South American dalliances in the 1990s, when Jim McLean turned to exotic markets to try and give his club a spark.

It began with the arrival of winger Walter Rojas in a £200,000 deal in August 1991. Weeks later it was the turn of forward Victor Ferreyra, an Argentinean international with a £350,000 price tag which equalled the club's record transfer fee paid for Michael O'Neill when he moved from Newcastle United to Tayside two years previously.

Both represented significant gambles but it was as though the manager had an itch to scratch after a previous aborted attempt to add a samba beat to the tangerine and blacks of Tannadice Street. The fascination can be traced back to 1988, when the veteran manager had made an audacious bid to sign Brazilian full back Josimar in the opening weeks of 1988. The defender had been one of the stand-out performers of the 1986 World Cup, scoring spectacular goals along the way, and was valued at £400,000 by his club Botafago.

That did not put off the ambitious Terrors, who made a formal approach before having to concede defeat to European rivals Seville, who could perhaps offer a more Latin environment than McLean and United could. It is, after all, the thought that counts and the Arabs had shown ambition in their efforts to land the Rio-born defender. He had been named the best right back in the world after his stunning introduction to the national team and overnight he became a global personality, moving just out of United's grasp. Josimar, by his own admission, got caught up in his celebrity and his career drifted after getting his big break in the European game. He may not have set the heather alight in La Liga, but the Tannadice fans would have welcomed the chance to have had a touch of World Cup glamour to add to David Narey's notoriety.

> "You're only given a little spark of madness. You mustn't lose it."
> **Robin Williams, actor**

Rather than the boy from Brazil, it was an attacker from Argentina that was entrusted with the role of adding flair to McLean's side in the early 1990s. Ferreyra had arrived from San Lorenzo in his homeland. He was reported to have played for his country and carried with him a great pedigree.

McLean was pinning his hopes on the South American contingent, sacrificing fans' favourite Miodrag Krivocapic after a fall-out with the Yugoslav. The eastern European defender had become a cult hero in his own right thanks to his classy displays at the back, an unruffled stopper with a cultured approach to the game and almost languid style. The fact he was a favourite with the fans did not prevent the manager from pushing him out of the door and it was Krivocapic's exit that freed up the work permit required for Ferreyra to begin his career in Scotland in earnest.

The cheque had cleared, the ink had dried and now it was time to discover whether the considerable outlay had been justified. Given the distance the new man was travelling, and presumably his total unfamiliarity with the Scottish game, it was a deal that represented a bold move on his part and that of the club he was joining.

He came from what may as well have been a different planet, having arrived in the relatively sleepy City of Discovery after years spent playing his football in the Buenos Aires neighbourhood of Boedo. With working-class roots and a history as something of an artistic hotbed favoured by poets and other performers, the district lent itself to passion and fervour on the football field.

San Lorenzo are one of five key teams in their home town, with Boca Juniors, River Plate, Independiente and Racing making up the group of renowned names in Buenos Aires. Accustomed to playing in front of crowds up to four times the size of those at Tannadice, Ferreyra found himself in far more sedate surroundings. He had bid farewell to a club on the up, one which went on to win the Argentine championship within four years of his departure. He joined a Dundee United side trying hard to maintain a challenge in the top half of the table as the 1990s proved to be far more trying than the previous decade.

He also arrived in a city a fraction of the size of Beunos Aires and its eleven million inhabitants, although Argentina's capital had not always been his home. Ferreyra was born inland in Rio Tercero, just a short hop from the hills of Cordoba. It was there that he learnt the skills that would find him gainful employment on three continents as a professional footballer. Along the way he courted controversy, stirred passions and was the subject of great debate.

Ferreyra made his debut in a 2-2 draw against Motherwell, but it was his second game that drew headlines. Ferreyra bagged a brace against Falkirk at Brockville to help his new side to a 4-0 victory as he joined Duncan Ferguson and Mixu Paatelainen on the scoresheet. McLean had a formidable forward line shaping up, with power from all angles as well as a touch of foreign flare from his new recruit to add to the developing blend. It would take a bit of time, but if he could continue to work on that special recipe, the end product would surely be a joy to behold.

In fact, goals from the Argentine attacker were few and far between. It was not until United played Falkirk again almost six weeks later that he made it onto the scoresheet again, this time in a 2-1 win, and then another two months until he struck lucky again in a 2-1 win against Airdrie. All in all there were five goals in twenty-three appearances, three of which were as a substitute, as the new man rounded off the campaign with the opener against Aberdeen in a 2-0 victory at Pittodrie in the closing weeks. It was a modest return on McLean's healthy investment, but in that time he had done enough to earn a place as a Tannadice cult hero. Some supporters went as far as sporting goatee beards in solidarity with a star they would label misunderstood rather than malicious, despite his brushes with authority.

The swarthy striker may have been a regular following his arrival in 1991, but when the 1992/93 season kicked off he faced a real battle to work his way back into McLean's plans. He mustered just a handful of appearances, mainly from the bench, before being packed off on his world travels once more.

He could at least console himself with the fact he had featured far more prominently than his compatriot Walter Rojas, the man who arrived amidst such great anticipation but turned out to be perhaps the greatest single letdown in the history of Dundee United Football Club. Rojas had been signed after receiving a glowing recommendation from a middleman trusted by McLean. It turned out to be a false reference, with a couple of reserve outings enough to convince the manager that he had been duped into signing a player nowhere near good enough to trouble his starting eleven. Indeed, it has been suggested a single training session was enough to prove that whatever footage McLean had seen to persuade him to close the deal was not of the same player that had arrived with his boots in hand. You win some, you lose some. Even McLean has been able to see the funny side of the Rojas débâcle in later years, although it is hard to imagine he was laughing too hard at the time. When he arrived from San Lorenzo, the same club that the more talented Ferreyra had been starring for, Rojas cost £200,000 and was hailed as a winger with ten caps for the Argentina under-21 side. Serie A champions Sampdoria and fellow Italian side Foggia were alleged to have been United's main competition for his signature and he carried dual-citizenship and an Italian passport enabling Rojas to sign without a work permit, cutting through the usual red tape. It may have been better if the authorities had blocked the deal since it proved to be an almighty blunder.

Rojas made two reserve appearances, both against Aberdeen, in the space of little over two months. A thigh strain was cited as the reason for his lack of match time and eventually he was sent packing. The saving grace was the £200,000 had not been spent upfront, with only a modest upfront fee paid on the basis that the rest would follow if Rojas made the grade. It's safe to say that he didn't.

The South Americans were dogged by controversy. For Ferreyra it took just three months for it all to unravel. It was in the run-up to Christmas in 1991 but there was no festive cheer when United travelled to Govan to tackle Rangers. In front of more than 41,000 supporters and the nation's television cameras, Ferreyra was seen to spit at home goalkeeper Andy Goram. The Scotland star was furious, the crowd was baying for blood and, with the incident missed by referee Brian McGinlay, it was left to McLean to step in. Ferreyra was substituted within a minute, but the controversy did not end there. As he left the pitch, the Argentinean crossed himself. It was a move that provoked an already volatile Rangers crowd to fever pitch. McLean insisted the spitting incident had not been behind his decision to withdraw his temperamental star from play, but his argument that the striker was fatigued appeared to be a touch contrived. The SFA swung into action while United also disciplined the player internally.

Unfortunately it was not the last time Ferreyra would draw attention to himself for all the wrong reasons. A player who was undoubtedly gifted appeared intent on self-destruct and alienating himself from his peers. In the eyes of most professionals there are few greater crimes than spitting at an opponent and the import had his card marked when he took aim at Goram.

To do it once could have been classed as reckless, an ill-judged act out of character. When it happened a second time there was no doubt that Ferreyra deserved to be derided in the way he was.

The repeat offence came at the end of the city derby in September 1992, the first time the match had been played in two seasons. Dundee had run out 1-0 winners in a match that had its flashpoints, including Duncan Ferguson's flailing elbow leaving Dens player-manager Jim Duffy requiring stitches. Duffy was also the man caught by Ferreyra's spitting in an incident missed by the referee. If the officials had not caught round one, they would certainly catch round two as Duffy and Ferreyra clashed at the end of the match after the Dundee boss had sought out his United opponent to exact revenge. Duffy has since claimed he would rather have been punched in the face than spat at and remains angry about the incident. He pointed out that he was swift to shake hands with Ferguson post-match, despite the physical scars he bore as a result of their tussle, but would never forgive Ferreyra. It was the after-match antics, in which the South American was seen to land a left hook on Duffy, that landed him in hot water with the SFA and he was not seen again for six weeks as a result.

By that time he had made noises about failing to settle in Scotland and the reaction from within the game to his latest faux pas on the park could not have helped. In mitigation he was 7,000 miles from home and operating in a style of football alien to that he had grown up playing in the Argentine domestic scene – but that could not excuse the worst of his lapses while in tangerine and black. Despite flashes of genius with the ball at his feet and some important goals, it is for the two spitting incidents that Ferreyra will be most remembered by the wider Scottish football public. He played only three more times after the match against Dundee, twice from the start and once as a substitute, before looking for a fresh start in a new land far away from the SFA disciplinary committee and any of the other parties he had managed to upset while in the Premier Division.

By January 1993 the short and rocky marriage had run its course. A number of clubs had made inquiries about Ferreyra's availability, not put off by the volatility he had displayed while at Tannadice, and with an all-important work permit at stake there was an opportunity to free up a place for another roll of the import dice. He had been complaining of homesickness towards the end of his time on Tayside, although opposition supporters had also grown tired of Ferreyra's approach to the game. His diving had brought a dressing-down from McLean, but in truth the manager must have had an inkling about what he was taking on when he plundered the South American markets in the first place. The phrase 'illegal simulation' was not even an inkspot on a referee's notepad when Ferreyra helped introduce the Scottish sporting public to the dark art; in those days it was classed as plain old cheating.

He left to join the Mitsubishi Motor Company team in Japan, or the Urawa Reds as they were renamed in the build-up to the first J League season in 1993. The club's preparations were dealt a blow when Ferreyra and fellow Argentine star Marcelo Morales departed early, heading for more familiar surroundings in South America. In the wake of the disappointment of that venture, the Urawa Reds followed a similar path to United in turning to more predictable players from Europe, with German names Michael Rummenigge and Uwe Rahn recruited to fill the void. Meanwhile, Ferreyra returned to his home country to play on with Belgrano Cordoba for two seasons. Spells back in Buenos Aires with Cordoba and Estudiantes and then back in Cordoba with Talleres followed before he returned to the capital city with Argentinos to play out his days as a professional.

Despite the lack of return for the money lavished on the Rojas and Ferreyra signings, the enthusiasm for enigmatic and mystique-filled South Americans did not fade on Tannadice Street. Early in 1995 Ivan Golac lured Uruguayan midfielder Juan Ferreri to windswept Scotland. He made a single appearance, as a substitute in a 6-1 win at home to Motherwell on 21 January, before dropping down to the reserves and never being seen again at first-team level. Ferreri had cost £200,000 when he joined from Defensor, with the twenty-five-year-old earmarked for a key role by Golac. He quickly grew disenchanted with the lack of opportunities at Tannadice, especially after Billy Kirkwood took over and did not see the import as part of his plans, and left the club at the end of the pre-season build-up to the 1995/96 season. He still had a year left to run on his contract when he upped sticks and returned home – making a surprise attempt at a Terrors comeback at the tail end of the 1995/96 campaign when he returned to the fold and started training with Kirkwood's squad again. The end result was the same though, with Ferreri failing to break into the team and ghosting away when his deal finally expired in the summer of 1996. He went home to rebuild his career with his old club Defensor but did spread his wings again at the start of the new millennium when he sampled Chinese football. Ferreri, capped twice by Uruguay, went back to the domestic scene in his homeland in 2001 and played out his career in South America.

At around the same time Golac brought Brazilian striker Sergio Gomes in from Portuguese side Amora. He became the first from his country to play professional football in Scotland but could not prevent the team from slipping to relegation. Gomes was more successful than many of his South American colleagues, winning a permanent place in the team under Golac and then his successor

Billy Kirkwood but finding it hard to hit top form in a struggling team. He managed just four goals in sixteen appearances and never reappeared in tangerine during the First Division effort the following term. Instead he continued his global quest by signing for Kuwait outfit Kazma.

There was also the mysterious case of Edison Machin, another of the Uruguayans to have tempted United. His arrival drew a crowd of thousands to a midweek reserve match but he never made it to the first team and disappeared completely off the radar amid reports that red tape had prevented him from returning to Scotland to take up United's contract offer.

Of course United are far from alone in being seduced by the allure of South American stars, ignoring the obvious differences in football styles and cultures between the two continents. Most Scottish teams have had them and very few have proven a success. Who could forget Rangers and their tribulations with Chilean striker Seb Rozental, the £4 million man who looked like a world beater until injury left him sidelined and he turned from hero to zero? Or how about Fernando Pasquinelli at Aberdeen? The Argentine striker, who had first landed on Scottish soil to play for Livingston, mustered just a clutch of games for the Dons before being sent packing after an unremarkable time in red. Celtic had their fingers severely burnt with the comedic recruitment of Rafael Scheidt and other forays into that most difficult of markets have proved equally disappointing. It was not only Rozental who stung Rangers, with Brazilian star Emerson generally proving a disappointment during a short and unspectacular period with the club in 2003/04.

Perhaps only Dundee, with the success of Claudio Caniggia and Co. during Ivano Bonetti's colourful reign, can claim to have had genuine success. But then, a World Cup winner, regardless of his off-field distractions, is usually a safe bet. Caniggia went on to spend longer than most South Americans in Scotland, being picked up by Rangers and having a positive influence at Ibrox in the way his compatriot Gabriel Amato had done in the 1990s. Amato, with his quick feet and deceptive skills, in many ways mirrored the qualities Ferreyra brought to the table.

What each and every South American import has had in common is a short-term relationship with the Scottish game. The lessons of the past have been studied, absorbed and noted by football club owners and coaches the length and breadth of the land – but it won't stop a club taking a chance in the future. Just as Jim McLean had his attention drawn to the promised lands, there will be many more in the years ahead who stake their reputation and cold, hard cash on the mysterious talents from the continent that brought us Ronaldinho, Ronaldo, Pele, Messi... and Rojas.

1993-1995
IVAN GOLAC

Magic Moment: After twenty years of hurt, Ivan Golac brought the Scottish Cup to Tannadice after leading the club in its sixth attempt since the first final appearance in 1974.

WHAT JIM MCLEAN achieved as manager of Dundee United was little short of miraculous. He took an ambitious club and made dreams come true. League Cup success, Premier Division glory and European credibility were all delivered to an appreciative audience. When it was time to bring his twenty-one-year reign to an end in 1993 it left a void of monumental proportions to fill and a conundrum for his fellow board members to address. So how do you solve a problem like Wee Jum?

The men entrusted with the task of coming up with the answer to that question were vice-chairman Doug Smith and director Bill Littlejohn. They had, on face value, what appeared to be an impossible job. Not only did they need to find a coach with the talent to follow on the heels of a man who had been a managerial messiah but also a candidate with the strength of character to cope with the bizarre situation of working under the previous boss in his role as chairman.

The saving grace for the club and its supporters was that they had pinned their faith in two men who were fit for the task. Smith

> "All of us, from time to time, need a plunge into freedom and novelty."
>
> **André Maurois, author**

is, after all, Mr Dundee United and somebody who could trump even the long-serving McLean in his dedication to the Tannadice cause.

From the moment he arrived at the club as a fresh-faced young man in 1959, Smith had never faltered. The cultured and cool defender became a lynchpin in Jerry Kerr's side of the 1960s and a key early ally for Jim McLean during his tenure in the 1970s. He was a captain who led perfectly by example. Famously never booked in 605 games as a top-class defender, Smith epitomised all that was great about Dundee United Football Club.

It was fitting that the Aberdonian's experience was not lost to the club and he went on to become a director, vice-chairman and, following McLean's subsequent departure from the top job in 2000, chairman of the team he loved. It was in his role as deputy to McLean at the head of the boardroom table that he took on the onerous task of pinpointing a new manager.

The usual long list of runners and riders began to circulate as the covert operation to unearth McLean's successor was mounted. Captain Maurice Malpas would have been a safe choice, a man steeped in the McLean traditions that enveloped the club. Fellow Arabs favourite Paul Sturrock was another familiar name in the frame, along with Jimmy Nicholl on the back of his efforts with Raith Rovers. Others quoted included Steve Archibald and English dark horse Steve Coppell. It was a big job and was creating big headlines, but Golac was a name that did not merit a mention until the surprise deal was struck to bring him to Scotland.

What Smith and Littlejohn did was a football masterstroke. They ripped up the rule book, ignored the obvious choices and instead turned overseas to find a man with the burning desire to bring the glory days back to Tayside. The process was thorough and exhaustive. Golac travelled to Scotland for hush-hush interviews before Smith and Littlejohn met with their chosen candidate at another secret rendezvous in Hungary, an appointment that required the prospective coach to make a 1,400-mile round trip by road as he dodged out of his war-torn country to keep his date with the Dundee United delegation.

Smith admitted that whoever he and his directors had appointed would have represented a gamble. Rather than going for a safe bet, they pushed the boat out and placed a risky wager on a runner from the back of the field.

The Tannadice stalwart told me:

'It was more or less left to Bill Littlejohn and myself to go through the process, Jim McLean made it clear he did not want to play a major part in it. Obviously it was an unusual situation to have the outgoing manager remaining in overall charge of the club and perhaps that made it more difficult in many ways.

'We had a list of applicants to work through, from home and abroad, but there was nobody who stood out as perfect for the job at that time. We were still considering the options when I went away on an international trip with the SFA and in conversation with Jack McGinn the name Ivan Golac cropped up.

'Jack told me that he and the Celtic board had interviewed Ivan for the manager's job at Parkhead. Although they went with a different appointment at the time, they had been impressed with Ivan. As soon as he mentioned the name I recognised it from our own set of candidates and when I got back to Scotland I spoke to the board about it and we decided to invite Ivan for an interview.

'He travelled over to speak to us, with Bill and I conducting the interview. We felt he came across very well indeed. You could tell immediately that he was a very outgoing person and a strong character, very much his own man. That felt like exactly the type we needed and the fact Jim McLean would still be in charge of the club really did not concern Ivan at all. He didn't know the chairman at all, whereas a Scottish manager coming in may have felt it was a tall order to replace Jim McLean.

'After the interview we reported back to the board and it was decided we should press ahead and make him an offer. Bill and I flew out to Budapest and met with him there to finalise the agreement. He had been keen to bring in his own assistant but that fell through for contractual reasons and Paul Sturrock remained in place.

'The impact he had in his first season was beyond our expectations. We had been to six Scottish Cup finals and had not won one, even though we probably should have done in at least some of those. For Ivan to win the cup at the first attempt was a dream start for him and meant a great deal to the club and the supporters.'

Golac made big promises when he checked in at Tannadice. He said:

'I believe in setting my sights high and I'll be aiming to win the lot. Sure it's a tall order, but I'm very ambitious and I'll be doing my best to catch Rangers – just as I'm sure my players will be. United are known the world over as a good football playing side and it's a reputation I want them to keep. But we must have the right mix of skill and steel. The flair has always been here, but we maybe weren't quite hard enough last season. I want them to be like I was as a player – very hard, but skilful too. I'll be aiming for a combination of the best of British and continental-style football.'

Golac admitted on his first day at the club that working with the previous manager as his chairman would be 'a little unusual'. It appeared the Serb had mastered understatement in the way in which he had perfected his neat line in disarming humour. While he could be acerbic and evasive when he wanted to be, Golac was a character it was difficult not to like for the media who found themselves wrapped up in Ivan the Terror's brave and bizarre new world.

He arrived with some pressing business to address. Duncan Ferguson's future as a Dundee United player was hanging in the balance after a summer of discontent. Leeds United and Rangers were both testing chairman McLean's resolve with multi-million pound bids that met with stony resistance. McLean the manager always hated losing prized assets to rival clubs. With Golac installed in the hot-seat, McLean the chairman eventually conceded defeat and cashed in on Ferguson's popularity by levering a £4 million fee from the Ibrox side.

The revenue generated from that record sale allowed Golac to carry out the club's record purchase, with the £600,000 recruitment of Serbian defender Gordan Petric months into Golac's reign. It was not his first signing, with Craig Brewster brought in for £250,000 and English journeyman Chris Myers also signed, but it was by far the most significant. For one thing it signalled the extent of the United board's ambition that they were willing to shatter the previous record transfer fee, which stood at the £350,000 spent on Victor Ferreyra and Michael O'Neill. Secondly it proved beyond all doubt that Golac was being given a free hand in the rebuilding of what was Jim McLean's squad.

Petric was very much a player in the Golac mould – unpredictable at times, unorthodox on occasion but with flashes of genius. The transfer was protracted but when the defender eventually arrived it looked as though it had been worth the wait, with some classy displays justifying his substantial price tag. The sight of the stopper embarking on mazy dribbles from his own penalty box and his apparently unflappable nature suggested entertaining days ahead for the United faithful. Of course he stayed less than two years before being sold on at a £900,000 profit to Rangers, but Petric proved that Golac had an eye for a player. His man of the match performance in the Scottish Cup final win against the Light Blues in 1994 no doubt sowed the seeds in Walter Smith's mind about a swoop for the cultured continental player. He breezed through the cup final, sharp in the tackle and able to turn defence into attack in a flash thanks to his precise distribution and willingness to break from the back with the ball at his feet.

Even before he managed to entice his main man to Scotland, the manager had instilled confidence in his own abilities. He had what some might describe as an impossible job as he attempted to fill the shoes of Jim McLean, who had guided the club to fourth spot in the Premier Division in his final season. Golac began by earning a 1-1 draw against Aberdeen in his first game in charge and that proved to be the start of an eight-game unbeaten run in the league. With three rounds of the League Cup also successfully negotiated in the first month of the 1993/94 season, it was a satisfying start to life in Scotland for the new man.

Defeat against Hibs in the semi-final of the League Cup and then an early exit from the UEFA Cup after losing out on the away goals rule against Brondby tamed the growing expectations, although the Scottish Cup run in the second half of the season stoked up the passion for the new manager. It took seven games to reach the 1994 final as, after edging past Arbroath in the first tie, it took replays to dispose with Motherwell, Airdrie and Aberdeen.

The cup run that culminated in that famous victory against Rangers at Hampden in the final did not distract from league business, with United finishing just inside the top half of the table in sixth place within the twelve-team Premier Division. It was, however, the manner and style in which he had led his charges to the Scottish Cup that captured the imagination.

There was an atmosphere of calm around the United camp in the build-up to the final. Rather than lock his stars away and spend hours trying to build a sense of tension, Golac led his men down a different path. He famously used to enjoy taking his players on walks in Camperdown Park and rather than embarking on a high-intensity programme during cup final week he halted what should have been the first training session to instead invite his squad to smell the flowers and soak up their surroundings. When the squad decamped to an East Kilbride hotel for the big game build-up there was no change in tempo. On the eve of the match he had his squad scatter to the Hamilton races for an afternoon of relaxation. Those who opted out of the jaunt to the turf stayed behind for a snooker tournament, with Golac trying his hand on the baize, before the squad reconvened for a few nerve-settling beers on the eve of the match as he fostered the spirit that ultimately proved so fruitful. He also let his men watch the final previews on television and used interviews with the Rangers stars as motivation for his troops, deducing from their words of wisdom that the big guns were rattled. Rangers, going for their second consecutive treble, were a team under pressure according to the rather more relaxed United boss. That was exactly the way it transpired as Craig

Brewster's goal rocked Rangers to the core and had the Arabs jumping for joy.

The problem for Golac was that after the smash hit of the trophy-winning first season, the next campaign proved a let-down. If he had been a musician, it would have been the equivalent of the tricky second album.

Wins were few and far between when the ball was set rolling in 1994/95. There were just eight victories in the first twenty-five top-flight matches and all of a sudden the hero was a dead man walking. The action was swift and decisive as Golac was dismissed and Billy Kirkwood installed as his replacement, but it was not enough to save the team from relegation. After the amazing adrenalin rush of the cup triumph just twelve months earlier, everyone connected with Tannadice had to deal with the crushing low of the drop down to the First Division. It was the end of a brave and exciting experiment that had ended in an honourable draw as the benefits of winning the cup one season were balanced against the financial consequences of relegation the following year.

Golac had arrived on a two-year contract but his stay was cut short when his ties with United were severed after twenty-one months working in the Scottish top flight. The decision was a mutual one according to the club statement, although the writing had been on the wall for the Serb as his relationship with McLean became more and more tense. Not that Golac let the strain show when he packed up his belongings and drove out of Tannadice Street for the last time. Instead he was in philosophical mood, claiming:

'I do wish more people would be happy in football. It is such a lovely game and the coaches should be more relaxed in order to have happy players out on the park. The game here is at a low stage and more flair on the field desperately needs to be encouraged. The pressure people are under has the opposite effect.'

Those enigmatic words came after Golac had met the chasing press pack at his Tayside home and, rather than slamming the door on them, invited reporters in for wine and whisky as he extolled his take on life in Scotland and his plans for the future. Many years later Golac spoke more candidly about the challenges he faced as McLean's successor, suggesting the chairman found it difficult to accept his cup success and share the joy that the club's first triumph in the national competition brought. Golac was perhaps stating the obvious when he claimed that he and McLean were 'totally different people when it came to football and life in general'. There was very little time to stop and smell the flowers when Wee Jum was in charge of team affairs and the contradictory styles must have done little to smooth the working relationship between the two men.

Doug Smith admits he was disappointed by the parting of the ways but would never apportion blame for the break-up in the relationship between Golac and the club. Smith said: 'The second season was a struggle. Ivan had a totally different style of management to his predecessor. That was maybe the problem in the end – he was just too different. There were only around eight games to go when the decision was made to get rid of Ivan, which I thought was a bit too late to be making a change. I still believe we would have stayed up if Ivan had remained as manager, but we will never know. It is difficult to pinpoint one reason that it didn't work out for Ivan in the long term. It was disappointing he moved on so soon, but football is like that.

'I still keep in touch and speak to him regularly. He's been back over to Scotland a few times since he left Tannadice and he's still the same character, such a nice person and so enthusiastic about football.

'There have been many managers brought to Scotland from overseas since then and very few have stayed for any length of time. The league set-up may be part of the problem, with so much familiarity between the teams because they face each other so often. The format was brought in for financial reasons rather than football and that has been to the detriment of the game at all levels.'

Golac's unorthodox and softer approach to the game was no reflection on his beginnings in the game. He came through the hard way and had to graft and scrap for recognition. The Serb coach was born in Belgrade in 1950 and rose to fame with Partizan in his home city, going on to star for Yugoslavia. In 1978 he made the break to the west when he joined Southampton and carved out a lengthy relationship with the south coast club. He was part of the Saints team defeated in the 1979 League Cup final against Nottingham Forest and made more than 150 appearances for the club. During eight years with Southampton the full back was sent out on loan to Bournemouth, Manchester City and Portsmouth as his experience of the British game grew.

Golac had a history of winning over British fans. When he first came to UK soil as a Southampton player, he quickly became a favourite of the crowd at the Dell. His brand of football was quick, skilful but aggressive. He was an overlapping full back who could attack and defend in equal measure, pulling no punches in the tackle but technically strong with the ball at his feet. He is remembered as one of the best overseas players to pull on the

Saints shirt, and there have been plenty over the years. He cost £50,000 when he was signed in 1978 by Lawrie McMenemy, who took advantage of the Yugoslavian rule that let players leave their home country only once they had passed the age of twenty-eight. Galatasaray had been interested but Golac was tempted away from Turkey by the prospect of playing in England. He played alongside household names including Kevin Keegan during his time in the south.

Every supporter loves a manager with the same passion for the cause as they hold themselves and in that respect Golac did not disappoint. A rebellious streak is cited as the reason for his modest collection of caps, with a series of conflicts with the Yugoslavian authorities blunting his chances of amassing a more impressive haul of international honours. He had a reputation as a tough tackling and combative defender in his day and he took those qualities into the management game as he got to grips with the hustle and bustle of life in Scotland's top flight. During one derby game, Golac attracted the ire of Dark Blues fans when he made a grab for a Dundee player and pulled him to the ground after encroaching into the United technical area as he tried to retrieve the ball for a throw in. It was the incident that inspired the 'magic hat' song dedicated to the unpredictable coach, a chant that has followed him ever since.

He had first taken a tentative step on the managerial ladder in the late 1980s when he returned to his homeland and took the role of assistant manager at Partizan Belgrade, stepping up to take charge when the manager fell ill and masterminding the club's celebrated victory over Celtic in the 1989 European Cup Winners' Cup. His team won 2-1 in the home leg before falling to a dramatic 5-4 defeat at Parkhead, a pair of results good enough to take them through at the expense of the Hoops, courtesy of the away goal rule.

The continental triumph put Golac back on the radar of British clubs and he was in the running for the Celtic manager's job in the aftermath of that result against the Glasgow side, losing out to Liam Brady. In the end it was not the big guns who came calling. Instead it was a return to his familiar south coast beat that beckoned, with lowly Torquay United proving an unlikely lure for the European coach. Never one to do things by the book, Golac appointed the maverick Justin Fashanu as his assistant.

The partnership lasted just a matter of months, with Golac putting the Torquay stint down to experience and returning home to take charge of Second Division outfit Macva and leading them to the promotion play-offs for the first time in their history.

It proved not to be his final crack at management in Britain and the Dundee United experiment provided him with that fruitful second chance. The cup success of 1994 did not convince the club that it was a route worth travelling down again when it came to replacing Golac. Deep in the relegation mire, they instead turned to a more conventional set of coaches to try and haul them back up the table. Veteran Gordon Wallace was at the helm with Paul Hegarty and Maurice Malpas by his side until Billy Kirkwood was installed in the manager's chair.

While Kirkwood battled to restore Premier League status after the inevitable relegation, Golac continued to lead a colourful life. His most recent football appointment took him to Libya in his capacity as the country's technical director. He had responsibility for every team from youth to Olympic level and remained in the chair until 2010, when he returned to Europe in search of his next challenge. Prior to his Libyan assignment he had served in

Iceland, Ukraine and his home country of Serbia while in his down time he divided his attention between homes in Vienna and Belgrade. Rather than the archetypal manager's pastimes of golf and long liquid lunches, Golac is happier spending his days on long walks in the countryside or indulging his passion for music and movies. Outside of football, Golac also had a stint in charge of a chocolate factory in Belgrade to add a new twist to an already eclectic CV.

Golac returned to Scotland in 2010 for United's successful attempt to regain the Scottish Cup for the first time since he held it aloft in 1994. He had also attended in 2005 when his old club were beaten by Celtic at the same stage of the competition. Just as he left a lasting impression on Tannadice, the Tangerines obviously made a big impact on the man from Belgrade. It also gave him a chance to meet with the Scottish media who he had enjoyed courting previously and, once again, he was ready and able to give them a line. Ivan, according to Ivan, was the man capable of picking Celtic off the floor following Tony Mowbray's disastrous tenure. He pitched for the job at Parkhead knowing in his heart of hearts that it was futile, but it was worth a shot. He was, after all, a Celtic fan deep down. He let his Dundee United players into that little secret during his time in charge and revelled in beating Rangers. Prior to one particular game against the Light Blues he promised the Glasgow side would be trounced by three or four goals. It was a bold and dangerous statement for any provincial club manager to make before a game against either side of the Old Firm – but he was true to his word, with his Tangerine dreams marauding into a 3-0 lead within the first twenty minutes of the Ibrox meeting in 1993. Golac had always been able to talk a good game and occasionally his prophecies came true.

The one prediction that nobody will ever be able to judge is the one that stated he would have won more trophies for United had he not been ushered out in 1995.

1993-1994

JERREN NIXON

Magic Moment: Rangers and their international defenders were toyed with and tormented as the Caribbean wonderkid was unleashed on an unsuspecting Premier Division in 1994.

Tangerines Career: Games 59. Goals 10. Caps 95 (Trinidad and Tobago).

H E WAS the £20 million man, £16 million man or £10 million man depending on which way the wind was blowing. All of those valuations were slapped on Jerren Nixon at different junctures by his eccentric manager Ivan Golac during his short stay on Tannadice Street in the 1990s. The price tags were fantasy, not that Golac would ever admit as much, but it all added to the intrigue and hype surrounding a player who might otherwise have slipped away quietly. Nixon found his manager's assessment of his worth amusing rather than a burden to be shouldered, shrugging off the rising figures with a wry smile as he played along with Golac's game. As with so many creative forces, Nixon was a confidence player and with Golac as his chief cheerleader there was no reason to lack self-belief.

"The glow of one warm thought is to me worth more than money."

Thomas Jefferson, American president

In full flight, Nixon was an attacking force to be reckoned with. Whether posted wide or through the centre of the United side, he had the pace and trickery to put supporters on the edge of their seats as well as the charm to bring smiles to the masses. The frustration was that the laid-back man from Trinidad and Tobago did not hit top gear often enough. In flashes, however, he showed glimpses of magic that led to the outlandish price tags plucked from the ether by Golac and fed to a press pack who thought all their Christmases had come at once with the growing clutch of unpredictable characters producing fresh lines on a daily basis.

The multi-million pound valuations served a dual purpose for the manager. For one thing they scared off any potential suitors who may have been tempted to test United's resolve with a more realistic bid for a flair player who still had his best years ahead of him. When Nixon signed in 1993 he had just celebrated his twentieth birthday and was undoubtedly a youngster with potential to go on to bigger and better things. The second purpose was to bolster self-belief in his young protégé and give him the impetus to fulfil his early promise. In the end neither proved successful in the long term, with the flying machine staying for two years and flitting in and out of the side before moving on for a far more modest fee than Golac had suggested might be achievable.

Nixon had arrived from Trinidad and Tobago, born in the village of Morvant near Port of Spain. Hailing from the home patch of West Indies cricketing legend Brian Lara, it was little surprise that it was with bat and ball that Nixon majored during his early years. Boredom spelled the end of the livewire's time as an aspiring cricketer, turning his back on the game because the tedium of fielding was too much to bear. That sport's loss was football's gain as the youngster threw himself into the beautiful game with spirit and passion. His childhood in the laid-back surroundings of the sunshine island coloured his personality, with Nixon's unassuming nature and beaming smile becoming trademark qualities during his years in Scotland. He was relaxed whether faced with a wall of fans or packed media room, always ready with a cheeky quip and seemingly at ease in any situation.

His talents were fostered as a teenager and he gained his first international recognition when he was called up to the Trinidad and Tobago under-17 side. Nixon went on to represent his country at every level up to and including the full side, making his debut at the top level in 1993 and playing on right through to 2004 on his way to a haul of ninety-five caps and thirty goals. He played a part in helping the Soca Warriors qualify for the 2006 World Cup in Germany but father time was against him in his bid to make the cut for the squad for the showpiece tournament and he missed out on a place on the plane.

It would not have been his first taste of tournament football on foreign shores. Playing in the the under-20 World Championship in Portugal in 1991 gave the youngster his first experience of football in Europe, although the European influence was not alien to any of the Soca Warriors players of Nixon's generation, having been born while the colonial rule of Britain was still fresh in the memory of everyone on the islands. It was not until 1962 that indepence from the Brits was achieved and 1976 when the Republic of Trinidad and Tobago became a reality born from a long-held dream.

Despite the relatively small catchment area, with the capital Port of Spain boasting a modest population of just 50,000 people, football on the islands is thriving. More than 200 clubs operate between Trinidad and Tobago, with a bustling amateur scene providing a feeder to the semi-professional set-up that has brought the world stars including Dwight Yorke.

Nixon's first club was the amateur outfit ECM Motown and he went on to play semi-professionally for Trinidad and Tobago Hawks as well as GT Cobra before earning his big break with Dundee United.

A select band of players from the Trinidad and Tobago under-20 World Cup squad of 1991 also went on to star in the professional game, with captain Yorke the most prominent of Nixon's contemporaries. Winger Angus Eve also ended up in England with Chester City, but the bulk never got the chance to earn a living from the sport. Nixon proved he had the drive and the talent to make a career in football and when he got his chance with United he did not hesitate in accepting the invitation to uproot from his homeland.

Although an unknown name in Scotland when he touched down to join Golac's rebuilding exercise in the City of Discovery, he was well on his way to stardom in his home country. His exploits with United won him the Caribbean footballer of the year title in 1994 and he won that prize again two years later, by which time he had moved on from Tannadice.

When Nixon arrived in Scotland he was faced with a steep learning curve. He was thrust into an alien environment against wily international players with a wealth of experience. One of his earliest tests was at Ibrox, introduced as a substitute against Rangers in April 1994. Nixon admitted after that match that he was shaking with fear when manager Ivan Golac gave him the nod to get involved in the match. That fear evaporated when he crossed the white line and within minutes of his introduction as a second-half substitute he was in full flow, terrorising a back four featuring the battle-hardened John Brown and Scotland stopper Richard Gough. It was Brown who was left trailing in Nixon's wake as he ripped through the Rangers defence to tee up Christian Dailly for the opening goal. It was a glimpse of what he was capable of in esteemed company. After that game Golac remarked: 'I told you before he was good, but he's not worth the £10 million I suggested. It's more like £15 million.' Nixon responded by claiming he would surely be worth £30 million before long. And so the legend of Nixon, the multi-million pound man, was perpetuated.

Pace was Nixon's most lethal weapon, with so many of the weary rearguards in the SPL left for dead as the entertaining forward hit top gear. Consistency was his downfall though, with Nixon making more appearances from the bench than starts as his frustrating dips in and out of form caused his manager a headache as often as his searing runs gave leaden-footed defenders a problem. It was very much a fifty-fifty split.

Nixon's first task was to acclimatise to his new surroundings, swapping the humid heat of the Carribbean for the swirling winds and biting cold of Tayside when he was lured across the Atlantic by the promise of a big break in the British game. Nixon's woolly gloves became part of his uniform at Tannadice, offering at least a sliver of protection against the elements.

His first competitive action was at home against Hearts on 8 January 1994, Scottish midwinter and as far removed from the land he left behind as is possible to imagine. Perhaps with the conditions in mind, Golac was cautious when it came to easing his new man into the fray. He spent half a dozen matches on the bench but spent long enough on the park in that time to convince his manager that he was ready for a starting berth. His big moment came at Easter Road against Hibs and Nixon responded by scoring his first goal on his first start, claiming the only goal of the game to emerge as the match-winning hero. With the No.9 on his back, the new man looked ready to prove himself as the answer to Golac's attacking prayers and with a goal in the bag it looked likely to be the start of something great,

It proved to be something of a flash in the pan, with that strike against the Hibees his only goal of the season despite eleven starts and eleven appearances from the bench across the second half of the Premier Division season, and the Scottish Cup campaign, in which he featured in all but the first of the eight ties up to and including the final victory against Rangers. Goals were not the sole reason Nixon had been brought to Tayside though and the menace he posed to opposition defences was reason enough for Golac to keep faith.

Basking in the glory of his status as a Scottish Cup winner, Nixon returned for the 1994/95 season bubbling with confidence. Golac, despite his lofty valuations, was clearly not convinced that his Caribbean craftsman had the hard core required for the Premier Division and used him as an impact player, with only occasional starts scattered among the weekly cameos from the bench. It was the same story when Billy Kirkwood took control in the wake of Golac's departure, as Nixon had to remain content with only occasional appearances in the starting eleven during the relegation struggle that term. In all he started thirteen matches in the league, Scottish Cup, League Cup and European Cup Winners' Cup during a year in which he made twenty-four appearances from the bench. He proved suited to the continental game, with a less frenetic pace than domestic encounters, and shone in what was an otherwise dismal European effort by Golac's side. Nixon played in both ties against Slovak side Tatran Presov and scored in both, although his strikes in the 3-2 win at Tannadice and 3-1 defeat in the away leg were not enough to keep the club in the competition. The Old Firm also brought out the best in the enigmatic star, with Nixon scoring against both Rangers and Celtic during the course of the 1994/95 season. Perhaps it was his ability to raise his game for the big occasion that drew attention from overseas, with Nixon's edited highlights no doubt making for impressive viewing.

He had become a popular figure around Dundee, settling on the city's Mains Road and sharing his flat with his girlfriend and his countryman Tony Rougier. Rougier by that stage was plying his trade across the Tay Bridge with Raith Rovers, part of a trickle of Caribbean players who made their way to the Scottish leagues during the 1990s and blazing a trail for another Tannadice fans' favourite in the shape of Jason Scotland.

Rougier, the powerful winger who went on to star for Hibs after making a significant impression with Rovers, became Nixon's sidekick and the pair blazed a trail for those who followed. Russell Latapy at Hibs, Rangers and Falkirk as well as Jason Scotland and Collin Samuel at Falkirk and then Tannadice have all brought flair to the SPL at various stages. The contrast between the West Indian culture and the urgency of the Scottish game could not be starker, yet the Trinidad and Tobago imports have all managed to shrug off the challenge of relocating to more hostile climes and without fail have brought a spark to every team they have represented.

When Nixon did depart Tannadice it was not in the multi-million pound deal that his manager had so confidently predicted. Instead it was a £250,000 offer that tempted United to sell, with the Swiss side FC Zurich tabling the bid in July 1995. The transfer was completed just eighteen months after the Trinidad and Tobago star had been brought to British shores for the same fee. The gamble in importing the unpredictable attacker had not paid off in the way Golac had originally hoped, but crucially Nixon left with the club not out of pocket and having brought a bit of sunshine to Dundee.

Nixon made a brief return to familiar shores in 1996 when he and his Trinidad and Tobago team-mates lined up against East Fife at New Bayview. It was an incongruous setting for the self-styled Soca Warriors, but a typically eccentric type of challenge match for the unpredictable international squad.

After Zurich he spent time with rival Swiss sides Yverdon-Sport FC and FC St Gallen, enjoying seven successful years on the continent and helping both Zurich and St Gallen into the UEFA Cup to add to the European experience he savoured with United.

That brought him back to Scotland in 1998 when Zurich were paired with Celtic in the second round of the UEFA Cup. The Alpine outfit were boosted by Nixon's intimate knowledge of the Scottish game and it was no surprise that he was at the heart of their team when they checked into Glasgow, helping the Swiss side to a 1-1 draw at Parkhead before coming on as a substitute in their 4-2 thumping of the Hoops back on home soil. That result suggested Nixon had not taken a step down when he opted out of Scottish football in favour of what so many had viewed as the football backwater of Switzerland and his mercurial talents transferred easily to his new surroundings. Nixon and his Zurich team-mates faced the might of Roma in the next round of the competition and were only edged out by the odd goal in five.

Following his time in Switzerland, the attacker took his career full circle and returned to the domestic scene in Trinidad and Tobago with North East Stars. He had retired from football when he returned to home soil, choosing the Caribbean as the base for his two young sons and putting his football ambitions to one side to make it happen. Despite interest from sides as far flung as China, he turned his back on the game and instead concentrated his attention on a new business, opening an electrical shop on his home island and looking to a future outside of professional sport.

It was after an approach from the Stars, a team which had been languishing at the wrong end of the league table, that his appetite for a comeback was whetted and it proved to be a decision that neither he nor his new team would regret as the revitalised forward set about transforming the fortunes of the Sangre Grande-based side. He was back playing for pleasure rather than pay and was back to the carefree spirit that had launched him as a player in the early 1990s, tormenting defenders on a weekly basis with the same pace that he had possessed when he burst onto the scene with Dundee United. He quickly became established as the most entertaining player in the Trinidad and Tobago league and enjoyed a successful new lease of life.

Nixon won the league and cup with Stars in 2004, a year in which he set a new record in his home country with a thirty-eight-goal haul in the league and was, not surprisingly, voted player of the year on the back of that performance. It was also the year in which Nixon, who was appointed captain of his club side, began his coaching career with the club before branching out into the youth game, founding the Nixon Soccer Academy in 2005 in the US city of Atlanta, passing on his experience to children between eight and twenty through his role with the academy, combined with a post as coach to the the Holy Trinity Preparatory School's teams in Georgia. Players between the ages of eight and twenty fall under the wing of Nixon now, with America providing the latest stop on a career which has taken him on a series of adventures across the continents.

Alongside him on the journey has been his wife, Kathy-Ann. Football is very much a family affair, with Mrs Nixon acting as co-director of the couple's football academy in the states as a fully qualified coach in her own right. Kathy-Ann also played at international level and rose to become captain of the Trinidad and Tobago women's team.

The duo are kept busy running their burgeoning academy but Nixon still makes time to follow Dundee United's progress from afar. His weekend ritual is to check on the club's score and, with two young sons showing football promise, he insists the Nixon name could yet reappear on a Tannadice teamsheet.

His own playing career took him across the world, but he still rates the Tayside excursion as the most enjoyable. The Scottish Cup win of 1994 is the one outstanding memory from an eighteen-month period that made a lasting impression on the quicksilver forward. His experience of working under the eccentric Ivan Golac was the other life-changing event, with the impressionable Nixon admitting he was too young to realise that the Serb, his first professional coach, did not always follow the management manual. The methods of his manager only added to the excitement and anticipation of his first paid-for football assignment and United provided him with a foothold in a profession that has served him well throughout his adult life.

1993-1996 and 2006
CRAIG BREWSTER

Magic Moment: Rangers dither but Brewster is sharp as the 1994 Scottish Cup is delivered in style by the Hampden goal hero who had swapped the terraces for the turf in time for the latest shot at glory.

Tangerines Career: Games 115. Goals 46.

HIS WAS the perfect football fairytale; the player left broken-hearted when his boyhood heroes released him as a teenager then fought his way back through the blood and thunder of the lower leagues to earn a second crack at living the dream. To cap the phoenix-like rise from the ashes of despair he scored the winning goal in the Scottish Cup final to take him soaring into the stratosphere with the legends of Dundee United's glorious past. Craig Brewster was proof positive that every story can have a happy ending if the leading man is willing to work hard to overcome the obstacles of adversity strewn across football's meandering path.

> "Victory is sweetest when you've known defeat."
>
> **Malcolm Forbes, publisher**

When the tenacious young pup Christian Dailly dispossessed Rangers goalkeeper Ally Maxwell inside the Gers penalty box in the 1994 showdown at Hampden and slammed his shot off the far post, the world stood still. For a split second it looked as though the chance to win a cagey encounter had gone – and then Brewster intervened to score the goal that has defined his career. Reacting first as Dailly made a menace of himself, Brewster rushed forward in support of his team-mate and was on hand to steady himself before side-footing home into an empty net from all of four yards to score the only goal of the game. He has scored far more spectacular goals and far more taxing ones, but never one more significant than that one on 21 April 1994.

With one swing of his right boot, Brewster ended an eighty-five-year wait for Dundee United to land the Scottish Cup. Both arms raised aloft, he stood lapping up the adulation of a delirious travelling support under the Glasgow sun as all of his wildest hopes fell into place in a split second of opportunism.

Guido van de Kamp, Alex Clelland, Maurice Malpas, Jim McInally, Gordan Petric, Brian Welsh, Dave Bowman, David Hannah, Andy McLaren, Brewster and Dailly ran out that afternoon aiming to knock the championship-winning Rangers side off their lofty perch. They did it and they did it in grand style. With Jerren Nixon joining the carnival as a late substitute, there were twelve players who went down in history as the first team ever to win the cherished old trophy for the club.

For Brewster it was a success story that he had good reason to be proud of. He knew exactly what it meant to the thousands of Arabs inside the national stadium that afternoon, empathising with the supporters who travelled to Glasgow with trepidation and excitement in equal measure. He had been a fan in the Hampden crowd for each of the five Scottish Cup final appearances previously and had left Mount Florida deflated and dejected. As a player he could at least influence proceedings and he did that to great effect on that wonderful afternoon, putting on a show for the friends and family who had flocked to the west coast to cheer him on. United had a ticket allocation of 12,000 for the final and Brewster had joked that he could have sold the lot himself.

If the demand for places in the stands was strong, then the clamour for places to welcome the victorious team back to the city centre with their coveted prize was even weightier. Thousands lined the streets to cheer on their men as they paraded the cup upon their return to Tayside and it was Brewster who received the loudest roar of the day as he held the cup aloft back on home soil after the successful mission in Glasgow.

Brewster had been released by Dundee United as a schoolboy and had to take a long road back to the team closest to his heart, serving an apprenticeship with Forfar and Raith Rovers before finding himself back in Tangerine in his late twenties. He joined Forfar in 1985 as an eighteen-year-old and spent six years at Station Park before moving on to Raith for a two-year stint and finally landing back at Tannadice in 1993 in time for the moment that has come to define his playing career.

Brewster told me: 'You don't quite realise at the time what effect it will have on you and your life. The day was an amazing experience. I'd been through five cup final defeats as a supporter and to be part of the team that finally broke that run and won the trophy was a great feeling. I was the fortunate one who scored the goal and that made it even more special.

'I was there from ten years of age but Jim McLean wouldn't call me up full time because I was never fast enough. I was with Dundee United as a part-time player until he freed me at the age of seventeen and I went to play in the juniors for two years. From there I had six-and-a-half years at Forfar as a ball-playing mid-fielder, either through the middle or on the left.

'It was Jimmy Nicholl who took me to Raith and turned me into a centre forward. If he hadn't seen that potential in me then who knows what might have happened. Luckily he did and I went on to score twenty goals for Raith, never looking back.

'When I went back to United it was Jim McLean's doing. I know it was at the start of Ivan Golac's time but I'm convinced it was Jim who was behind the signing. I went into the team playing wide on the left and didn't do particularly well, having not had any real pre-season training. After that first game I don't think I made another appearance for the next twelve weeks. When I did come back into the side I scored against Partick and kept my place after that, scoring twenty goals that season in thirty-seven games. It was a great time for me and obviously culminated in that afternoon at Hampden.

'I think a lot of Dundee United supporters stayed away because they thought there was no chance we would win. Like me, they had sat through final after final and all of them ended in defeat. On top of that, Rangers were going through their dominant phase. What happened that day showed that nobody has a given right to win cups, not even the Old Firm.'

The striker had Scottish Cup pedigree even before his day in the sunshine at Hampden. He was a sales rep in the less than glamorous world of waste disposal during his days as a Forfar Athletic player when he flirted with heroism, leading the Loons line against Celtic in the 1989/90 tournament and stunning the Hoops with a well-taken free-kick goal just three minutes into the tie at Station Park. He gave the Forfar fans hope that their side was about to pull off one of Scottish football's greatest shocks but those dreams were shattered when the Parkhead side scored twice to edge through to the next round. The Glasgow giants left it late though, with the Angus minnows holding them at 1-1 until an eighty-fourth minute free-kick from Jacki Dziekanowski clinched a lucky win.

The forward's story was almost the dream that never was. His long-awaited move to Tannadice looked set to become reality in the summer of 1993 when he went on trial with Ivan Golac's squad and impressed the Arabs boss enough to earn a contract offer on the back of two years of great service with the Kirkcaldy outfit. The stumbling block was that terms did not match those on offer from Raith and the whole deal was in danger of collapsing until common ground was found and the paperwork was completed to push through his £250,000 switch from Stark's Park.

His first season as an Arab proved unforgettable. He made the No.10 shirt his own, scoring sixteen times in thirty league starts, and added four goals in the Scottish Cup run to break the magical twenty-goal barrier. He was the first player to hit that target since Iain Ferguson in 1987.

His performance against Rangers in the cup final drew attention to Brewster and he began to be linked with big-money moves, with Norwich, seeking a replacement for Blackburn-bound Chris Sutton, among those reported to be waiting in the wings with cheque book at the ready. The popular Dundonian did his best to dispel the rumours, pledging his future to the Tannadice cause and vowing to pick up where he had left off when the new season kicked off. Preparations went well, with a hat-trick against Stoke City in pre-season giving him the perfect boost as the competitive action loomed.

If the first campaign had been a fairytale, the second could only be described as a nightmare. Brewster's goal touch deserted him and United were on the ropes, eventually falling out of the Premier

Division after propping up the ten-team top flight. He scored just eight goals in the league, cups and Europe that term.

The striker remained key to a swift return to the big league, banging home seventeen goals in thirty-two league and play-off appearances as United returned at the first attempt. He was not around to savour the promotion for long though, departing at the end of his contract in the summer of 1996 and landing a surprise move to Europe when Greek side Ionikos came calling.

Brewster up to that point had appeared to be a stereotypical Scottish centre forward. At 6ft 1in tall he was the 'big man' that every team wanted up top. Strong and good in the air, Scottish teams did not look for much more. When he disappeared from view in 1996 nobody thought much more about it until he returned in 2001 with Hibs. Brewster of old was gone and in his place was a new, improved version. He was toned, tanned and wiser for his experiences abroad. There was a new subtlety to his approach, with an apparently never previously exploited ability to link play with all the prowess of a *libero*. He still had an eye for goal but had added new strings to his bow during his Greek assignment, not least an obsessive interest in fitness and conditioning that allowed him to roll back the years and put many of his younger team-mates to shame.

He had immersed himself in the culture of his new country while playing for Ionikos, a relatively young club with less than forty years of history behind them when he signed. They had begun to establish themselves in the country's A-League but were by no means one of the giants of the Greek game, more of a pocket dynamo with big ideas and the benefit of a wealthy benefactor to help them along their way. The Scot became a huge hit with his new side, helping them to push forward in the Greek top division and into the UEFA Cup for the first time. Brewster's goals also helped the team realise its dream of appearing in the Greek domestic cup final during his time with them. In return he was given a new outlook on diet, fitness and tactics.

All good things come to an end and in 2001 it was time for Brewster to return to base, with Hibs the destination. He arrived in Leith as a thirty-four-year-old but showed no signs of flagging, with the same enthusiasm evident as when he was patrolling Tannadice five years earlier.

Brewster spent a year at Easter Road before linking up with Jimmy Calderwood at Dunfermline, a manager who had sampled continental football himself as a player and who could appreciate the finesse that the time in Europe had brought to his new recruit's game. At various stages there were calls for a late Scotland call-up for the refined and experienced attacker, but that proved to be one of the unfulfilled ambitions of his career.

Months into the 2004/05 campaign it was time for a new chapter to be written as Brewster the player became Brewster the manager, taking charge at Inverness Caley Thistle and helping to keep the Highlanders in the Premier Division in the wake of John Robertson's defection for Hearts. He developed a reputation as a sparkling young coach, bringing a steely organisation to the Inverness side and a fitness drive that harked back to his Ionikos days. He turned to his former Hibs colleague Malky Thomson as his assistant, having watched at close quarters as Thomson built a reputation as a fine young coach at Easter Road. Thomson went on to work at Celtic and then Rangers before pairing up with Brewster as he began his managerial odyssey.

The pair steadied the ship after their appointment and the unrest created by the change in management, and steered the

Highlanders to eighth place in their first season as an SPL club. They had flirted with a top six position but ended the campaign happy to have consolidated their place among the elite, finishing eight points above Dundee United and proving that a big budget was not always necessary to enjoy relative success. In addition to Thomson, Brewster installed Peter Davidson as fitness coach in Inverness as his empire began to build.

The results were clear to see for his admirers at Tannadice. At the start of the 2005/06 he took his north upstarts down to Tayside and held big-spending United to a 1-1 draw. Then he dumped them out of the League Cup after masterminding a 2-0 victory and continued to hold the advantage in the SPL, recording a further draw to remain unbeaten against his old side. In between he also helped the plucky Caley Jags to a series of other big results, including a win at Hibs and draws against Rangers and Aberdeen. With every unexpected point, his credentials were growing more attractive to prospective suitors.

Before anyone else could take advantage, United chairman Eddie Thompson acted swiftly. Just as the path from Forfar and Raith led him to his spiritual home on Tannadice Street during his playing days, the route back to Tayside appeared preset once he embarked on a managerial career. The big moment came in January 2006, when Thompson invited the Scottish Cup-winning hero back to Dundee United to take the top job. It cost in the region of £250,000 in compensation, roughly the same fee United had paid to bring Brewster to the club as a player all those years previously, but Thompson had never been frightened to back his convictions with cold hard cash and felt the price tag was worth paying.

For Arabs it was the return of the prodigal son. Nobody questioned the appointment and Thompson was praised for his ambition, coming to a decision that brought supporters out in their numbers to give Brewster the hero's welcome that he was always likely to receive. Here was a man who had the club at heart and who had, in his short time as a manager, proven himself to be a strong leader.

The chairman wanted him to succeed, the fans wanted him to succeed and the new manager was desperate to succeed. Unfortunately it did not have a happy ending and less than twelve months after he had walked back through the front door, Brewster was ushered out again.

He had adopted the same approach at Tannadice as he had at the Caledonian Stadium, supported once again by trusted lieutenants Thomson and Davidson. He immediately pledged to get tough with the underachieving Arabs players and set about initiating double training sessions and extra work in the gym. It had paid dividends at his last club but did not have the same impact back 'home'.

The run to the end of the season and the start of 2006/07 was full of frustration. After just a single win in the first twelve matches of the SPL, Brewster was given the heartbreaking news that his big shot with his boyhood heroes was over. The saving grace was that his relationship with the United supporters had withstood a torrid period and he left with his dignity intact. Infact, Brewster has since classed his exit as a blessing and a relief.

He had been a victim of circumstance as much as anything, taking on the challenge at a time when the belt was being tightened by Thompson after his heavy spending of previous years had failed to yield a return on the pitch.

He was forced to shop in a different price bracket from his predecessors and had some success. Among his recruits were Lee

Wilkie and a certain Craig Conway, lured from Ayr United. Having played a starring role in the 1994 Scottish Cup success, Brewster in his own way had an important part to play in helping to piece together the jigsaw for the 2010 triumph.

Conway was his parting gift to United, leaving in October 2006 and tempted back to a playing comeback by Jimmy Calderwood at Aberdeen. Not for the first time, he proved there was life in the old dog with some sparkling performances with the Tangerines. He showed the Pittodrie youngsters how it was done and looked like a man with a weight lifted from his shoulders, free from the burden of management and able to get back to his roots.

Brewster said: 'I went to United at a bad time. They had to beat our Caley Thistle team on the last day of the previous season to stay in the SPL, so they were not in a position of strength. I went back to Tannadice in January 2006 and left in October that year. In between I signed Noel Hunt, a player the club has since made a lot of money on, as well as Craig Conway and blooding David Goodwillie – who are both attracting interest from bigger clubs at the moment. I also took Lee Wilkie to the club as well as Steven Robb and David Proctor, so you could argue that four out of six was not a bad return in terms of the success of those signings.

'The club had gone through a period of spending a lot of money for very little return and when I arrived the policy was changing. I only had one transfer window to work in and it was a case of trying to put building blocks in place – it is impossible to change the type of run United had been on overnight.

'In the end it was a relief when I got out of Tannadice. If the opportunity to go at that stage hadn't come up, who knows what would have happened for me. You can't say whether it was the right decision or the wrong one, but if I hadn't taken the job at that point it may never have come up for me again. I would like to think I left Dundee United in better shape than I found them.'

Just when life looked simple, the phone rang. It was Caley Thistle, looking for a replacement for manager Charlie Christie. And so the merry-go-round span again and the well-travelled Dundonian was heading back up the A9 to try and pick up where he had left off in the Highlands.

He returned in August 2007 as the unanimous choice of the board, who had been impressed by the way he handled his departure previously. There had been no animosity and there was an acceptance in Inverness that there was no way they could have stood in the way of Brewster when his first love came calling.

The stage looked set for him to breeze back in and regain his confidence in the dugout, but the script did not have a happy ending. Just as it could be argued Brewster should never have gone back to United, the same applied in the north. His second spell at the Caledonian Stadium lasted sixteen months and his final season, in which he left the club four months before the conclusion, ended in relegation for the Caley Jags. He had left when the team were rooted to the foot of the table and his successor Terry Butcher could not arrest the problems that blighted Brewster's second stint in charge.

The United hero dropped off the football radar to regroup and recharge his batteries before being brought back into the game as a player by Ross County in 2009, and that brief assignment led to a place on the coaching staff as assistant to Derek Adams. He had once attempted to sign Adams for Caley Thistle, but the tables had turned full circle.

The job with the Dingwall side led to the emotional reunion with United in the 2010 Scottish Cup final at Hampden. Not surprisingly Brewster was a man in demand during the pre-match media scrum, a headline writer's dream as he aimed for his second success in the national competition.

Brewster said: 'The memories were brought flooding back because everyone knew what had happened in 1994 and wanted to talk about it. I was born in Dundee and scored the winning goal for my team in the cup final – it was a great story, so I can understand why people want to talk about it even after so many years.'

The man responsible for Dundee United's only Scottish Cup triumph up to that point was now one of the men who stood in the way of them collecting the trophy again. Adams, Brewster and the rest of the County team earned plaudits for their incredible journey to the final, shocking Hibs and Celtic along the way, but fell at the final hurdle when they could find no answer to Peter Houston's spritely Terrors in Glasgow. United had failed to read the script and the underdogs could do little but roll over in the face of an accomplished display at Hampden.

The County assistant boss said: 'I had said all along that if we could produce a performance on the day like the one we did against Celtic in the semi-final then I would be a very proud man indeed. In the end we didn't produce that level of performance – mainly because United didn't allow us to.

'It was still a run that gave everyone a lot of satisfaction. We scored nine in one round and then beat Hibs and Celtic. Any team doing that fully deserves to be in the final. For over an hour we held firm and then we were undone by a fantastic finish by David Goodwillie.'

Good grace had always been a Brewster trait and he was magnanimous in defeat that day, just as he had been pragmatic when it was time to clear his desk at Tannadice. He is the first to admit he has unfinished business as a manager and it appears certain that before long Brewster will have the chance to put right the wrongs of his most recent postings in Inverness and Dundee.

KJELL OLOFSSON

Magic Moment: Champions-elect Rangers are humbled 1-0 on their own Ibrox turf in 1999 and Olofsson is the man who puts them to the sword. Once again he proves to be a man for the big occasion.

Tangerines Career: Games 119. Goals 46.

THE 1960s brought Finn Dossing, Lennart Wing and Orjan Persson hero status at Tannadice. The 1990s brought Kjell Olofsson, Erik Pedersen and Lars Zetterlund, as the second coming of the Scandinavians and they reaped a similarly rich harvest for Dundee United fans. Olofsson and Pedersen in particular did their bit to roll back the years and ignite vivid memories of the swinging sixties for those old enough to remember the first wave of imports from Europe's northern outposts.

Finn Dossing was tall, athletic and had a deadly eye for goal. Kjell Olofsson displayed all of those hallmarks and in doing so gained the love and respect of the Tannadice faithful. Orjan Persson was a cultured midfielder with the same technical brilliance that made Zetterlund a hit a generation later, while Wing's commitment was mirrored by the dogged and determined Pedersen while he was on his way to form a special bond with the tangerine masses.

Olofsson was signed for the not inconsequential sum of £400,000 from Norwegian side Moss in 1996 by Tommy McLean, and arrived at the club with that big price tag to justify. It did not take him long to do just that and soon he had repaid the sum several times over with his rise to become one of the most prolific forward players of the modern era at United.

Love Is In The Air has become an Arab anthem, but the origins can be traced back to the time of the Viking invasion of the 1990s. With the lyrics adapted as a tribute to the new striking sensation, with variations of 'Olof's in the air' or 'Olofsson's in the air' being belted out by the Shed boys' choir, it became part and parcel of life as a United fan. The player moved on and the song reverted to the original lyric, peaking at the 2010 Scottish Cup final when tens of thousands joined together for an emotional rendition of the tune. It was also released as a single for the cup final, but the impromptu live performances at grounds up and down the country are what have really captured the imagination and the Hampden version was a class apart. A certain Kjell Olofsson was in the middle of the thronging mass of Tangerine that day, no doubt recognising the familiar melody from his days playing in front of the passionate Dundonians. He was joined at the final by Zetterlund and Pedersen, no doubt reliving their own shot at cup glory. The Hampden return was far from Oloffson's first appearance on Scottish soil since his playing days ended and he even appeared dressed as the club's mascot, Terry the Terror, during one game at Tannadice to lift spirits.

> "Love is in the air, everywhere I look around."
>
> **John Paul Young, musician**

It was during the 1997/98 season that the trio helped United to the final of the League Cup and although beaten 3-0 by Celtic in the final at Ibrox it was a run to remember for all of the players involved. The Scandinavian trio were ever-present in the five ties in the competition, joined by Sieb Dijkstra and the defensive duo of Mark Perry and Steven Pressley.

It was a tough road that McLean's side followed and they had to overcome some considerable obstacles to reach the showdown with the Hoops. After breezing past Queen of the South there were ties against Hibs, Rangers and Aberdeen to negotiate before the final could be contemplated. The Hibs tie, in which Zetterlund was on target, went to extra time before Gary McSwegan settled the match at 2-1. The quarter-final tie against Rangers also went to extra time before McSwegan scored another dramatic winner and against Aberdeen at Tynecastle in the semi-final it was a tough shift to secure a 3-1 victory in which Robbie Winters notched a double and young Craig Easton scored another. That effort in the most difficult passage to the final imaginable set up the showdown with the Parkhead men in Govan and almost 50,000 turned out to ensure a carnival atmosphere. Despite the 3-0 outcome, it remained an experience not to forget for all of the United players who carried the hopes of their club on their shoulders that day and marked another milestone for manager McLean after the success of qualifying for Europe the previous season.

McLean took charge after a horrible start to the 1996/97 season cost Billy Kirkwood his job, with five defeats and a draw from the opening six league matches of the campaign. The new manager had no time to ease his way into the job and needed instant results. He went out and brought in Olofsson in a bid to turn the fortunes around and scored an instant hit. He leapt to the head of the striking queue, pushing Robbie Winters down the pecking order and effectively deeming the youth product surplus to requirements.

The new man scored his first goal in only his second appearance, in a 3-1 victory at Motherwell, and from that point on was a regular contributor as United charged up the Premier Division table towards an impressive third-place finish despite the testing start to the term. He started twenty-two matches and scored twelve goals in the league, finishing top scorer ahead of Winters.

By the time the 1997/98 season kicked off he was just hitting his stride. In the first dozen Premier Division matches he netted ten goals, including a wonderful week in which he scored a double to help his side to a 3-1 win against Hibs at Easter Road and then another brace in a 5-0 demolition of Aberdeen at Tannadice. He went on to score eighteen league goals in thirty-two appearances and another four from four starts in the Scottish Cup as well as one against CE Principat in the UEFA Cup. That twenty-three goal haul elevated Olofsson to his place as a hero.

A further eleven goals in his third and final season proved McLean was right to invest so heavily in the experienced frontman. With his physical presence he stood apart from most in the top flight, but Olofsson was about far more than just height and strength. He had touch and instinct to add to the mix and the ruthless streak every great striker needs.

Olofsson had his progress hindered by a knee injury during the 1997/98 season, requiring cartilage surgery. Not that the operation kept him sidelined for long as the dedicated Swede worked away during gruelling solo sessions in the gym to propel himself back into the first-team reckoning far quicker than either he or his manager had expected, rushing back to unexpectedly play in the Scottish Cup quarter-final and responding by scoring a double against Celtic. It was still not enough to clinch a place in the next round, with the Hoops winning 3-2 courtesy of an injury-time own goal from Erik Pedersen. It was the best of times and worst of times for Pedersen, who had rushed to Tannadice to play in the game just hours after his wife Beate had given birth to their son.

The departure of Tommy McLean and arrival of Paul Sturrock in his place threw Olofsson's future into grave doubt. He had been a McLean signing and assured of a place under the veteran coach but Sturrock had other ideas, not frightened to drop the Scandinavian within weeks of taking over the top job.

It was not that Sturrock did not rate Olofsson, more that he was already looking to a future without the tall forward. His contract was due to expire and without an agreement for an extension in place, Sturrock would have been happy to have swapped the hitman for a lump sum before he was free to walk away for nothing.

There were rumours of a bid from Preston North End and talks aimed at striking a contract extension, but in the end neither bore fruit. Instead he walked away at the end of his contract in the summer of 1999 and returned to his old Norwegian outfit Moss. In the end Sturrock's best offer was not enough to tempt the fans' favourite to stay for another year, rejecting a bumper wage at Tannadice in favour of a move back to the family home he had kept in Norway and the security of a job outside of football for when his playing days ended. The decision came in February 1999 but the popular Swede made it clear to Sturrock that his commitment to the cause had not wavered and he remained an important part of the squad through to his departure that summer. Indeed, Sturrock claimed the attacker's form improved once the doubt about his future had cleared and he was able to focus solely on playing out the final weeks of his time at Tannadice.

Aberdeen's Danish manager Ebbe Skovdahl attempted to lure Olofsson back to Scotland in the autumn of 1999, just months after he had left Tannadice. The loan deal was close to becoming reality but the Dons pulled the plug at an advanced stage of the negotiations because they were not willing to wait for the end of the Norwegian league season to conclude the short-term switch.

Pedersen had joined from Norwegian side Viking Stavanger in 1996 at the same time as Olofsson, making his debut alongside his fellow Scandinavian in a 1-0 win at home to Hearts. He remained a mainstay of the side under Tommy McLean that season on the run to a well-deserved European place and in the 1997/98 season, his first full campaign as a United player, was only outdone by Sieb Dijkstra and Lars Zetterlund on the appearances chart.

Pedersen left United in the summer of 1999 and returned to his homeland with the wonderfully named side Odd. He was linked with a return to the British game with Bristol City, but his hopes were dashed when the English side's Norwegian coach Benny Lennartsson parted company with the club and instead it was Odd who succeeded in landing his services on a two-year contract.

His career at Tannadice had been brought to a premature end when he first suffered a knee injury February 1999 and then the added complication of a blood clot in the region of the initial knock after minor surgery, which had been designed to get him back to fitness more quickly than if it had been left to heal naturally. Pedersen was desperate to get back to playing for his beloved Arabs but had to concede defeat when specialists advised him that he would be at serious risk if he did go against their diagnosis that it was not safe to return to action. He had already missed a chunk of the campaign due to a pelvic problem, a crushing blow for a side in dire need of the type of drive Pedersen brought to the table. The pelvis injury, caused by inflammation on the bone, eventually led to a double hernia operation to cure the pain he had been playing through – claiming at times it felt as though someone had stuck a knife in his stomach. Still he played on, trialling various medications to combat the pain.

Manager Paul Sturrock paid tribute to his attitude and commitment but urged Pedersen to heed medical advice. He also knew that Pedersen's decision to quit the club, hot on the heels of Olofsson's announcement about his plans, would hit the Terrors' support hard but claimed in the Bosman era there was little he or the board could do. Gone were the days of Jim McLean when terrace favourites could be tethered to the team for five years at a time. Just as had been the case for Olofsson, the choice was all about returning to Scandinavia to settle with his family after the adventure in Scotland. It did not prevent him from raving about his time in the land of tartan and heather and he was among the first to recommend a move to Scotland for compatriot Thomas Solberg when he had the chance to move to Aberdeen under Ebbe Skovdahl.

Pedersen had never been shy of speaking his mind no matter what the topic was and at one point had to explain himself after apparent criticism of manager Tommy McLean had appeared in a Norwegian press report. According to Pedersen he had in fact been critical of disciplinary standards in the Scottish game and it was an explanation McLean was happy to accept from a player who wore his heart on his sleeve – not to mention the club badge, which he now has tattooed on his right arm as a lasting reminder of the time he spent on the east coast.

To this day, Pedersen proudly displays the tangerine and black crest, no doubt bamboozling plenty of the uninitiated back in his home country. Explaining the decision to make the permanent tribute to the club he loved, he said: 'I wanted something that truly meant something special to me – and that was United.'

The distinctive body art was just one of Pedersen's quirks that has earned him everlasting hero status. While on the playing staff he would greet supporters as he ran from the tunnel, geeing up the United faithful with passion that inspired confidence and returning at the end of games to celebrate or commiserate. He connected with the crowd in a way that not all imported stars have been able to do, immersing himself in Tannadice life and becoming one of the family. For a man from foreign climes, he did a good impression of a lifelong Dundee United supporter. Except it wasn't an act, as Pedersen remains an ardent Tangerines fan and was in the crowd for the 2010 Scottish Cup victory to cheer on the team as an honorary Dundonian alongside Olofsson and Zetterlund.

Zetterlund had departed Tayside in March 1998, becoming the third and final member of the Scandinavian contingent to confirm his plans to depart at the end of the season, with Swedish side Orebro agreeing to pay a nominal fee to take him back across the North Sea before the end of the campaign. He had fallen behind David Hannah in the team order and Paul Sturrock also saw new recruits John Eustace and Neil Murray as preferred midfield options, leaving no room for the Swede. Zetterlund admitted at the time that kicking his heels on the sidelines had been driving him crazy, causing him to question his own ability and contribution to the cause. It was time for a clean break before any more damage could be done.

He had been a familiar figure for Tannadice fans for well over a decade – having gone from villain, as a member of the IFK Gothenburg side which defeated the Tangerines in the 1987 UEFA

Cup final, to a hero as part of the team that took United back into European competition in 1997. In fact, it was Zetterlund's goal against Motherwell in a 1-1 draw at Fir Park at the tail end of the 1996/97 season that secured third spot and guaranteed a UEFA Cup place.

Zetterlund, who had played for AIK Stockholm and Orebro after starting out as a teenager with Gothenburg, had been a calming influence in the United midfield, credited by youngsters such as Craig Easton as one of the major influences on and off the park in their development. He was composed, competitive and an intelligent player who never let his team down.

The one display that epitomised Zetterlund more than any other came in the Sottish Cup in September 1998 when the Tangerines faced plucky Second Division opponents Caley Thistle in the last sixteen of the competition. The Highlanders had pegged the Premier Division favourites back to 2-2 after Tommy McLean's men had surged into a 2-0 lead. The potential for a massive cup upset was very real until Zetterlund stepped forward with a spectacular eighteen-yard drive in extra time to finally kill off the Caley Jags challenge and put his club through to a quarter-final tie against Celtic. Zetterlund's relentless probing from the middle of the park took its toll, with the midfielder being physically sick when he got back to the dressing room after a tireless shift in a match he described as 'like no other' he had played in. He had felt ill during the game but soldiered on to play a hero's role, admitting afterwards that his sickness could quite as easily have been down to nervousness about the impending embarrassment of a cup exit as it was to anything else. He felt the pain of the supporters who were on tenterhooks as the hopes of a cup run threatened to evaporate in front of them.

The tie had already gone to a replay after the first meeting had ended locked at 1-1 and for the demanding Swede it was simply not good enough. He used the post-match press conference to issue a very public apology to the Arabs who paid good money to watch their men toil against the outsiders from the lower leagues.

He had arrived at the same time as Olofsson and Pedersen, drafted into the side a week after the other pair, and then not budging from the team for the remainder of the season. He was not flashy nor did he pose a goal threat, but Zetterlund had a metronomic ability to control the pace of a game and keep United ticking over in the most testing of circumstances. In the hurly-burly of Scottish football, players with the intelligence and ability to put their foot on the ball and retain possession were worth their weight in gold.

Off the field he also adapted well to life in Scotland, joined by his wife Ylva and daughter Kristen for their new life in the city. He extolled the virtues of Tayside and of his new employers, claiming Tommy McLean's tough but knowledgeable persona made him the perfect manager to play under. All in all, life could not have been any better for the imported midfielder as he set about making the most of the opportunity to sample a new culture and new sporting environment at a relatively late stage in his career.

The common theme with all of the Scandinavians was their ability to take to Scottish football and life in the country without fuss or failure, a lesson first taught by Jerry Kerr and his 1960s recruits. The modern-day Viking invasion was no less successful and created a new set of heroes for the Tannadice faithful to enjoy.

2005-Present

DAVID GOODWILLIE

Magic Moment: With a fleeting glance and a subtle brush of the boot, Ross County's cup dream was in tatters and the Arab celebrations began.

Tangerines Career: Games 88. Goals 20. (To summer 2010)

W HEN ROSS County goalkeeper Michael McGovern elected to leave his box to head clear a long through ball in the 2010 Scottish Cup final against Dundee United there was a flutter of anticipation in the tangerine and black section of the Hampden crowd. When his clearance fell toward David Goodwillie thirty yards from goal, the hearts skipped another beat. When one of the youngest players on the park chested the ball with the composure of a Brazilian World Cup winner and proceeded to loft the sweetest of lobs over the despairing Highland keeper and two lunging defenders on the goal line the pulses went into overdrive and the celebrations began. Love really was in the air, and it was Goodwillie who was the object of the affections of the rapturous United fans.

> "Believe and act as if it were impossible to fail."
>
> **Charles Kettering, inventor**

Then, amid the bedlam, came the most touching moment of the afternoon as Goodwillie, so often portrayed as the bad boy of Scottish football, lifted his strip to show a top bearing the message 'For You Nana'. It was a tribute to his late gran, who had passed away before getting the chance to see the apple of her eye hit the heights as a footballer.

The goal not only showed Goodwillie's sensitive side, a world apart from his cocksure persona, but also the professionalism that has helped his rapid progress. A booking from the referee was the reward for his heartfelt celebration. The perfect lob, it transpired, was no fluke. It was a technique he had spent hours on the training ground trying to perfect in the weeks leading up to the final. None of those practice shots had made the net bulge, but when it mattered most he was able to dig deep and make it count. It really was a goal fit for any occasion and the fact he had the guts to go for goal, rather than the plethora of safer options in front of him, marked Goodwillie out as a player with the temperament to play at the highest level.

Craig Conway's two excellent goals put the icing on the cup final cake and ensured the emphatic 3-0 victory that took the famous old trophy back to rest on the Tannadice sideboard for only the second time in more than a century of football at the club.

The abiding memory for most from that final will be of the ball sailing through the air and falling towards goal. The arc of the Goodwillie shot appeared to take an eternity to be drawn in the Glasgow sky, but when it completed its path the eruption inside Hampden brought the spectacle back into real time after the freeze-frame effect of the striker's audacious effort.

He, like Craig Brewster before him, is assured of immortality in the tangerine half of Dundee. He is also guaranteed a permanent place on the Scottish football record as one of the most promising players produced in modern times, having won the SPL Young Player of the Year Award in 2010 even before his cup final heroics.

While the Liverpool bound Rangers stopper Danny Wilson went on to scoop the Scottish PFA and Scottish Football Writers'

Association prizes, in which Goodwillie was also among the frontrunners, it was the Arab who got the nod at the league ceremony. To some of the uninitiated outside of Tannadice, it was a curveball and a departure from the traditional Old Firm dominance of the end-of-season gongs. For those who watched Goodwillie blossom at close quarters it was fitting recognition of the work he had put in to take himself to the next level.

The big question is whether that development continues at the same pace and whether it continues at Tannadice or elsewhere. As Hibs have discovered, keeping young talent at a club outside of Scotland's big two is often an impossibility. Just as the Easter Road side lost Scott Brown, Derek Riordan, Steven Whittaker and Kevin Thomson to the Old Firm there have already been whispers that the same conclusion is inevitable for United and Goodwillie.

In the summer of 2010, as Rangers attempted to build for the future, the rumours of a £750,000 bid from Ibrox began to intensify. Tannadice chairman Steven Thompson was swift and decisive, publicly stating that he had no intention of selling his star man for that type of derisory figure. He was pragmatic enough to admit that if the right bid was tabled he would have little choice but to consider it and bold enough to go on the record with his valuation of Goodwillie. That figure is £3 million and represents a measure of the esteem in which the chairman and his manager hold the Scotland under-21 international. That hefty price is surely more than cash-strapped Rangers could contemplate, perhaps a tactic designed to put them off completely rather than drive up the likely revenue. When Thompson claimed he had no desire to sell, it felt like a genuine sentiment echoing that of every fan who willed the ball to drop over the line during the Hampden festivities in May 2010.

If Goodwillie is tempted to look for greener grass elsewhere, he would be well advised to consider the experiences of Duncan Ferguson. Physically the two are poles apart, with the small and nimble Goodwillie different in stature and style to the tall and powerful Ferguson. Size excluded, the parallels between Goodwillie and Duncan Ferguson are incredible. Both grew up in Raploch, the Stirling community renowned for its tough environment. Both found an escape through football with Carse Thistle boys' club and both had their talents spotted by Dundee United rather than any of the senior teams closer to their central belt base. Both quickly rose through the ranks at Tannadice to become first-team stars while both have also had brushes with the police that have brought unwanted attention. The big question that remains to be answered is whether Goodwillie will follow in the footsteps of Carse Thistle's most famous former player and be plucked away from Tayside while his career in tangerine is still in its infancy.

It is impossible to say what would have become of Duncan Ferguson if United had stuck to their guns and knocked back the advances from Rangers. His time in Glasgow was obviously marred by off-field events, but his impact on the pitch failed to live up to expectations.

While Ferguson became a cult hero with Everton, the club where he finally found a football home, there has to be a sense of regret for the Dundee United supporters who watched the raw and exciting talent thunder onto the scene in the 1990s that he did not exploit his potential to the full. After joining Rangers early in his career it appeared a case of 'too much too young' as he struggled to cope with his status as Scotland's big-money man and with his role in the Old Firm soap opera.

The challenge for everyone connected with the club now is to ensure that Goodwillie does make the most of his talents and that he continues to thrive and mature. The second part of that task it to keep hold of the latest Raploch starlet long enough to complete the process.

According to Dick Taylor, the founder of Carse Thistle and Ferguson's mentor in his early days, the new boy in town has the ability to go on and become a Scotland international as well as hitting the heights in club football. Taylor, who coached Goodwillie as a teenager just as he had done with Ferguson, admits he has not been as excited about a young prospect since Big Dunc began to make a name for himself. According to the Carse stalwart, Raploch's gritty nature is part of the reason his young charges have the hunger and attitude to set themselves apart from the crowd. That attitude has helped Goodwillie succeed where so many young players have foundered.

My first sight of Goodwillie was when he appeared for United's under-14 side in a youth cup final against Hibs. It was Sean Fleming who stole the show that afternoon with a match-winning volley, but Goodwillie was also on target against the Edinburgh kids and clearly had potential, even at that young age. Since then I've monitored his progress through the under-16 side and then up the ladder and into the first-team squad, although it would be wrong to say he looked marked down for greatness from the moment he signed. Goodwillie has been part of successful Arabs age-group squads but he has galloped ahead of his peers from those early days.

Capped at youth level by Scotland, he was a regular scorer at under-16, under-17 and under-19 level for his country before he had kicked a first-team ball at club level. One of the highlights was a hat-trick against Bosnia for the under-19 side in his home town of Stirling in 2006 as the national team began its European under-19 Championship qualifying campaign, while he also scored the winner against Germany during the same campaign.

At club level his debut came as a substitute against Rangers at Ibrox at the end of 2005, introduced by Gordon Chisholm during the death throes of his managerial tenure. It was after Craig Brewster had taken charge early in 2006 that the striker notched his first goal, when the sixteen-year-old became the youngest ever SPL scorer when he hit the mark against Hibs at Easter Road. He had something of an Indian sign over the Hibees, with all three of his first SPL goals coming against them. Months after his first goal he signed a three-and-a-half-year contract extension as United protected their prized asset from possible predators.

It was as Craig Brewster plotted a summer clearance in 2006 – informing Derek McInnes, David Fernandez, Paul Ritchie, Jim McIntyre and Grant Brebner that they were free to leave the club – that Goodwillie and fellow young hopefuls Ross Gardiner, Stuart Abbot, David Robertson and Greig Cameron began to stake a case for permanent promotion to first-team duties.

Brewster challenged the group to prove they were the answer to his recruitment headache as the gaps began to show in the elite squad, but he did not get to harvest the fruits of his labour. When Craig Levein came in as Brewster's replacement the youngster had to set about proving himself all over again.

Levein was wary of over-hyping Goodwillie, playing down his potential as a ready-made first-team player. The manager's former Leicester City sidekick Kenny Black, by then in charge of Airdrie United, attempted to sign the young striker on loan for the Diamonds in 2007. That bid was rebuffed but in time for the

2007/08 campaign Levein deemed it was time to send out his boy to be toughened up among the men of the Scottish Football League and it was Raith Rovers, led by former Hearts coaching colleague John McGlynn, who benefited from the decision. Goodwillie became an integral part of the Stark's Park side and thrived during his time in Kirkcaldy.

He made his entrance for Raith at Stark's Park on 29 December 2007 and got off to a flying start when he scored after just five minutes in a Rovers shirt, putting his team on the path to a 3-2 victory against Alloa in the Second Division. It was the same result when Goodwillie scored next, against Cowdenbeath in a Fife derby. He also scored a crucial double in another 3-2 win, this time at Ross County, as well as the only goal of the game against Airdrie in the latter stages of the season. In all, he scored six times for Raith to help push them into the play-offs, where they missed out on promotion following defeat over two legs by Airdrie.

He returned from his time in the Second Division with experience at the coal face and was firmly lodged in Levein's plans for the 2008/09 campaign, a cause helped when he scored a double against Cowdenbeath in the League Cup on his first appearance for United that term. He proved to be something of a lucky charm, with his side never losing when he found the back of the net. Another goal against Airdrie United took them through to the next stage of the League Cup while contributions home and away against Hibs brought a 2-2 draw and 2-1 win. His sixth and final goal of the season was at home to Aberdeen in a 1-1 draw in the SPL. His goals in the early stages of the League Cup had been vital to the run that took the club all the way to the Hampden final, although by the time the match against Celtic was played the youngster had been relegated to the stands. He was able to watch and learn from his seat at the national stadium, locking away elements of the occasion for his own chance on the big stage in 2010. The fact United had run the Parkhead favourites so close that afternoon, only defeated after the marathon 11-10 penalty shoot-out effort on the back of 120 minutes of tense football without a goal, sowed the seeds that silverware was a realistic possibility for the young side being moulded by Levein.

The only glitch was that Goodwillie has not always been the model pupil whilst learning his trade at Tannadice. In 2008 he was fined by the courts after a scuffle in a Stirling nightclub and just a year later was back in court after a similar incident in a Bridge of Allan nightspot. Both were viewed in a dim light by his employers, with the latter punished heavily by Craig Levein with a club fine since it happened on the eve of a training session and therefore conflicted with the Tannadice code of conduct. Levein admitted he was 'extremely disappointed' with his young star, but there was no over-reaction by the club. Instead there was a measured response and the opportunity for Goodwillie to prove he could mend his ways and keep out of trouble.

He responded in the best way possible as he became a central figure in the 2009/10 campaign. Danny Cadamarteri, with all of his Premiership experience, was the man all eyes were on as the campaign unfolded but it was Goodwillie who soon began to grab the attention.

While the newly recruited Englishman got off to a flying start, he was soon overtaken by Goodwillie in the scoring stakes. Thrust into action from the start of the season, the young Scot got off the mark against Alloa in the League Cup and went on to net thirteen times to finish joint topscorer at Tannadice with Jon Daly. Along the way he proved a man for the big stage, scoring at Parkhead early in the campaign when Celtic were held to a 1-1 draw, as well as in some intensely pressurised cup duels. The run to the Scottish Cup final at Hampden was punctuated by Goodwillie's regular goals and consistently impressive displays.

Despite his tender years he has already displayed a maturity and understanding of the game. Coupled with tenacity and all-important pace, he has already been tipped to go on and play for the international team if he can remain focused on football.

In the cup run of the 2009/10 season he scored in the 2-0 win against Partick Thistle that set the ball rolling and followed up with the only goal of the game when St Johnstone were knocked out in the next round. David Robertson was the match-winning hero against Rangers in the quarter-finals but Goodwillie was back on track in the semi-finals when he settled the nerves with an early opener against Raith Rovers. It paved the way for a 2-0 victory and a date with destiny at Hampden the following month. Having missed the previous cup final there was a burning desire to be involved this time round and on the back of a superb contribution over the course of the season there was never any likelihood of him being sidelined.

And so it came to pass, Peter Houston sent his men out to do battle with Ross County as the honour of being Scotland's cup supremos was laid on the line. The coach kept faith in his young striker and Goodwillie did not disappoint with a display that mirrored those he had been producing all season long. In a marathon campaign he played forty matches, a statistic only bettered by Prince Buaben, Craig Conway and Sean Dillon. The final was by no means a classic, with both teams content to play a spot of tactical chess in the first half, but it was United who enjoyed the better chances and who always looked in control.

DAVID GOODWILLIE

With young livewires such as Goodwillie and Conway pressing forward at every opportunity, resistance appeared somewhat futile for the Highlanders and eventually they cracked when the sixty-first minute effort flew into the net. It is a goal that Goodwillie will find defines his career and even his life as the years roll by and the magnitude of his achievements sink in.

The season represented a coming of age for Goodwillie as a football player and he stood up to be counted with some big performances at big stages in the season. None was bigger than the Hampden date and together with Craig Conway he thrilled his appreciative followers who had waited a long time to see their team once again get their hands on the prize. To win 3-0 against a club that had already accounted for Hibs and Celtic was above and beyond all expectations.

How far Goodwillie goes, and whether he remains a Tannadice Idol or exits as a villain in the style of his Raploch forefather Duncan Ferguson, is entirely up to him. Whatever happens he will always be remembered as a cup-winning hero. Just ask Craig Brewster.

2007-Present

JON DALY

Magic Moment: With both hands raised in the air, Jon Daly's goal celebration matched those of the United supporters. In an instant, Put Your Hands Up got the seal of approval from the man himself.

Tangerines Career: Games 79. Goals 24. (To summer 2010)

FEDDE LE GRANDE may sound like a half decent continental centre half but in fact his contribution to the Dundee United cause has been in a strictly non-playing capacity. The Dutch DJ is one of the men behind a modern Scottish football phenomenon and Jon Daly is his unlikely partner in crime. Blend the two seamlessly together, add in a few thousand exuberant Arabs and you have the perfect anthem: 'Put Your Hands Up For Jon Daly'.

Of course neither of the key protagonists had a direct involvement in it but surely neither could have predicted the catchy chant, to the tune of Le Grande's hit *Put Your Hands Up For Detroit*, would become the overnight sensation it has. In an era in which football crowds have become sanitised to the point of becoming anodyne, the brilliant adaptation of the hit has breezed a breath of fresh air through the Scottish game, put a smile back on the faces of crowds home and away and proved the Tannadice faithful to be top the SPL's chart.

Various renditions in a plethora of settings have made their way onto *YouTube* and tens of thousands of people have viewed them as the cult of JD grows with every passing week. At the time of writing, the most popular video of the Daly tribute by Arabs fans, recorded at the Scottish Cup final in 2010, had attracted close to 10,000 hits. The next most-watched Daly video has been seen close to 5,000 times and all in all the trail of clips has hauled in an incredible number of football followers from all over the world. It has spread far beyond football grounds though, with impromptu performances springing up in nightclubs and bars across the city and transmitted through *YouTube* to reinforce the message. Daly himself has embraced the worship from the stands, catering his goal celebrations to join the 'Put Your Hands Up' dance with his adoring army of fans.

The phenomenon extends beyond the music and straddles the world of fashion. In the weeks leading up to the cup final the ArabTRUST produced a run of t-shirts sporting the 'Put Your Hands Up For Jon Daly' slogan and a silhouette image of the player and Arab devotees. Needless to say, the design proved an instant sell-out when released for sale in city centre music store Grouchos. Subsequent batches have continued to be snapped up as the Daly bandwagon rolls merrily forward, gathering momentum and adding strength to the cult status of a player who arrived as a relative unknown but who will check out of Tannadice one day in the future as a hero.

> "If you love what you are doing, you will be successful."
>
> **Herman Cain, author**

The fans who dote on their Dubliner will be hoping that day is later rather than sooner but when it comes he will at least be able to say that he has put something back into the club. The profits from the t-shirts have been ploughed back into the United youth academy, just one of the fundraising efforts masterminded by an organisation which is now the second largest shareholder in the club. Established in 2003, ArabTRUST has raised tens of thousands for club coffers since its inception but has also given ordinary supporters a vehicle for making their voice heard through the group's place on the club's board.

The trust is perfectly placed to tap into the Tannadice zeitgeist and the Daly t-shirts have hit the mark in spectacular fashion, latching onto a football trend that stems back to the early 1990s, when Vic Groves, the Arsenal star of the 1950s, provided the inspiration for a new wave of sporting apparel. Gunners fan Alan Finch decided to ditch his polyester football kit and seek out a local dressmaker to produce a replica of the shirt made famous by Groves. Little did Finch realise his retro request had created a business monster. Soon he had quit his career in the music industry and founded The Old Fashioned Football Shirt company, or TOFFS as it is better known to football fans across the globe. The empire began in his dining room, with just Finch and his wife as the team behind it, but now is based in a Newcastle factory with a staff of thirty and a multi-million pound turnover.

The company is servicing a seemingly unquenchable thirst among lovers of the beautiful game for a slice of the past, earning contracts with clubs and international federations across the globe, and has provided its distinctive cotton kit for countless films and television productions. But the real appeal of TOFFS is not on the playing fields and games halls of Britain; it is on the high street and in the bars of every major city in the land.

Football fans, it seems, have gorged themselves on an endless diet of man-made modern replica strips but tastes have developed and refined over time. Now the supporter wants something different, something distinctive. In 2011 TOFFS will celebrate its twentieth year and in the cyclical world of football fashion a new trend has emerged to rival retro, with an even more subtle approach paying dividends for enterprising companies seeking a slice of the pie.

In 2004 a Glasgow firm by the name of Fitbo Europe appeared on the scene, marketing a 'Legends of Football' series of screen-printed t-shirts. Plain old retro replica had been replaced by a line of products with a clever twist, borrowing from popular culture and adapting to suit the football niche.

A succession of companies have piggybacked onto the success of what began as a niche product and ArabTRUST has cut out the middle man, creating a product for fans designed by fans.

Trust chairman Stephen Simpson explained:

'Nobody can really say where it came from, but obviously the song was around and fresh in everyone's minds. Then Jon did a bit of a silly celebration at the end of a game, waving his hands above his head, and the two of them were married together to make the "Put Your Hands Up" chant. It became self-perpetuating.

'The t-shirt was a resounding success, even though one or two people weren't convinced that it would work. We're fortunate that we have Kevin Goghan at Tayprint supporting us, he does all of our design and printing for the t-shirts we produce. We will give him an idea of what we're looking for and Kevin, a big United supporter, goes away and produces three or four design ideas for us to choose from. Quite often he'll say just take ten or twenty of a particular design and see if it sells, that way there's no big financial risk. It was just the same with the Jon Daly t-shirt but as soon as the initial run went on sale they sold out. So we took another 100 and they sold out. Then another 100. We kept ordering in 100 batches because we thought demand would run out, but they kept selling. In the very short space of time between the first one being produced and the cup final we sold more than 900 tops.

'At around the same time, Ian Cathro from the youth development department came to the trust and said they needed to attract some funding. We decided then and there that all of the proceeds from the Daly t-shirts would be directed to the youth academy and I think that encouraged supporters to buy them.

'It was also fortunate timing from our point of view, with a lot of people who wouldn't normally buy merchandise looking for something to wear to the cup final at Hampden. When the last ones sold in the summer of 2010 we decided not to reprint them because we feel it has run its course and it was time to do something fresh.

'The challenge for the trust is to keep coming up with new ideas for merchandise and to keep people interested. It would be easy to keep selling the same things, but before long people stop looking. On the back of the Jon Daly success we have to come up with the next idea, although it was made slightly easier by the fact we had the option of using the Scottish Cup in the designs. That was an obvious route to go down and was always likely to be popular.

'A large part of our remit is not just to raise money but also to do whatever we can to help the club in other ways. Most recently we have helped to organise the programme sellers, relying on our members to give up their time to join in on match days as well as looking for others who, although maybe not willing to stand outside and sell programmes, could deal with the logistics of that whole operation. By reducing the number of staff the club needs to employ we're putting something back into the club and helping them to tighten its belt.

'We have around 1,000 members, although that figure includes those who have bought one-off children's memberships as well as the adults playing the annual fifteen-pound subscription. Those junior members are obviously older now and are potentially new subscribers. Our task is to determine how many active members we have on that list. There is a hardcore of fifty supporters who attend every event but there are many others who don't.

'We've put on some excellent events, everything from traditional dinners to "Meet the Manager" sessions, and it would be great to be able to attract the whole trust membership out to these. In the current climate it's a real challenge to raise funds but we are soldiering on and coming up with new ways to keep people interested wherever possible.

'The trust has been running for around ten years now and we're fortunate that the club does listen to us. We have a seat on the board as an associate director and that in itself is a big step forward. Because the club is operating with a small board, it means that our own influence is heightened because we have a quarter share of the vote. We are taken seriously by the board and are able to make a positive contribution.'

The trust is also intent on making Tannadice a fun place to watch football, embracing the spirit echoing around the stands. The distinctive tangerine Jon Daly t-shirt has become a feature in the stands but has also been brought to a worldwide audience courtesy of Cameron Kerr, the avid Arab who has become a familiar figure in club colours at the World Snooker Championship at the Crucible over the years. When Neil Robertson won the title in Sheffield in 2010, Kerr took advantage of his front-row seat for the Australian cue star's celebrations by doing a swift rendition of the 'Put Your Hands Up' dance in front of the BBC lenses as the camera followed Robertson around the arena. Kerr was, naturally, wearing his 'Put Your Hands Up' t-shirt for his impromptu television performance of the routine.

The dance may have been lost on large swathes of the viewers who tuned in for the snooker, but in a corner of Scotland it struck a chord as the devotion to Daly continued to manifest itself in weird, wonderful and brilliant ways. Even Lorraine Kelly, celebrity fan extraordinaire, has got in on the act and been pictured putting her hands up for Jon Daly... with a rather bashful-looking Jon Daly pictured beside her. It's not easy being an idol, but the striker has done his best to take it in his stride and, during press interviews, has even made reference to the buzz he gets from seeing the supporters with their hands aloft in celebration of his goals.

Kerr's Crucible display came as the Scottish Cup final against Ross County loomed but the Irishman's position as a fans' favourite was secure long before the glorious run to Hampden. That campaign and subsequent triumph against Ross County only served to reinforce his place as Tannadice's favourite son. The sight and sound of the massed ranks of United supporters joining together at Hampden has been captured for all time on the internet as a lasting memento of the impact the big Irish striker has had on his adopted home in Scotland.

It is not only *YouTube* on which Daly has reached a worldwide audience. Tribute pages on social networking sites including *Bebo* and *Facebook* have also popped up as the supporters bid to take their love of their modern-day hero to as wide an audience as possible in any way they can. Thousands have signed up to join those internet groups and the numbers show no signs of slowing in the wake of the cup triumph. It appears there is a never-ending stream of Arabs wanting to put their name to the trails of support for the unlikely hero.

Born in Dublin, Daly's career was decidedly unremarkable before he pitched up at United in January 2007. He had begun his professional career with Stockport County before moving on to Hartlepool, via loan stints with Bury and Grismby Town, but struggled to pin down a regular place at any of those English sides despite a more than decent scoring return. In one week alone at Hartlepool he bagged seven goals over the course of three games – yet was still deemed a player the club could live without. That incredible run of form, in September 2006, began with doubles at Peterborough United and Grimsby and was rounded off with a hat-trick at home against Wrexham. A job well done, but months later he was shipped off to Scotland to start afresh with United.

One club's loss proved another's gain as he went on to find a permanent home in the SPL and fulfil the promise that had originally tempted Stockport to lure him across the Irish Sea from his amateur side Cherry Orchard. He had been taken to England as a teenager having represented the Republic of Ireland at under-14, under-16 and under-18 level and went on to play for his country's under-19, under-20 and under-21 sides.

Despite a meandering start to life as a professional, Daly was at the top of wily manager Craig Levein's shopping list when he took charge and was one of his first recruits. He arrived just days before his twenty-fourth birthday, looking for a spark to ignite his career, and checked in with words of praise from Levein ringing in his ears. According to the manager he was the perfect target man, tall enough at 6ft 2in to provide a physical menace yet mobile enough to pose a goal threat into the bargain.

His debut did not go to plan, making his first appearance in a 5-0 reverse against Rangers at Ibrox. His first goal came more than two months later but was worth waiting for, with Daly grabbing a last-minute equaliser against Celtic at Tannadice when he cancelled out Shunsuke Nakamura's opener. A goal against Aberdeen at Pittodrie, in a memorable 4-2 victory, helped ingratiate Daly further in the eyes of his growing band of supporters but a knee injury cut him down just as momentum was building.

Stephen Simpson recalls: 'The funny thing is that Jon didn't start very well when he joined the club. He didn't do too much in the games he played and missed quite a few through injury too. I would go as far as to say the supporters were beginning to turn against him when he scored with a wonder-strike against Celtic to equalise in a game at 1-1. That goal began to change opinions and then in the Scottish Cup-winning season he peaked at the right time, scoring some vital goals but also producing some very good performances.

'He is really an unlikely hero. If you had asked any of the supporters at the start of the 2009/10 who the star player over the next nine months would be, I don't think Jon Daly would have featured high on the list. He came through to prove everyone wrong and give himself a real chance of becoming a club legend. Whether he can make that transition is very much up to Jon and whether he can stay clear of the injuries that have been a problem for him.'

Despite bad luck with injuries, Daly was awarded a three-year contract extension at the tail-end of 2008 as he committed himself to the cause until the end of the 2011/12 campaign. A second serious knee injury and then an ankle injury sent the Dubliner back to the treatment room and at stages he feared his

Dundee United days were numbered. He spent months in rehab alongside Lee Wilkie, who by then was facing what appeared to be his inevitable retirement. With familiar grit and determination, the striker battled back to fitness and forced his way back into the side and right into the middle of the Hampden mix for the 2010 Scottish Cup final. Daly has admitted there were dark days when he wondered if he would kick a ball again, but those thoughts could not have been further from his mind when he lined up at Hampden against Ross County in the biggest game of his career up to that point. Watching the pain and emotional turmoil Wilkie faced when he had to give up the game only served to heighten Daly's determination to make the most of his own opportunities and the cup campaign was his moment to shine.

He was there every step of the way during that marvellous run, starting every game, from the opening fixture against Partick Thistle right through to the climax against Ross County. Daly was one of five men who featured against Thistle, then St Johnstone as well as both matches against Rangers in the quarter-finals, Raith Rovers in the semi-final and County in the final. Goalkeeper Dusan Pernis, Prince Buaben, Morgaro Gomis and final hero Craig Conway were the others.

Although Daly did not net in those cup ties, he proved the perfect foil for strike partner David Goodwillie.

Craig Levein's role in creating a cup-winning cult hero cannot be underplayed. It was Levein who brought Daly to Tannadice but more importantly it was Levein who put the club on the firm footing that made the Daly success story possible.

From the day the 1997/98 season ended with Tommy McLean's side toiling just three spots off the foot of the table to the arrival of

Levein in 2006 there was an air of gloom around Tannadice only lifted by fleeting moments of optimism.

In the ten-team Premier Division there were ninth- and eighth-place finishes in 1999 and 2000. In 2001, when the SPL came to pass and the twelve team set-up should have given breathing space, it was no better as United clung on for eleventh spot. Eighth spot in 2002 hinted progress was being made under Alex Smith but it was back to eleventh in 2003. The top six finish under Ian McCall in 2004, when the young boss led his charges to fifth place, and the run to the Scottish Cup final under his successor Gordon Chisholm in 2005, when Celtic won 2-1, proved to be false dawns. In 2006 and 2007 the best United could muster, by then under Craig Brewster, was ninth.

Levein swept in and began to put all of the experience mustered during his apprenticeship at Cowdenbeath, Hearts, Leicester City and, briefly, Raith Rovers to good use.

At last there was solid and consistent progress and Daly was central to that and his manager's plan. United, for so long the soft touches, had a new physical presence to give a hard edge that made them difficult to beat and a team no side relished playing against.

Gone were the relegation struggles and instead came the push for European places, with fifth-place finishes in 2008 and 2009 as well as the agonisingly close call in the 2007/08 League Cup when only penalties, after a 2-2 draw at the end of extra time, could separate United from winners Rangers. Daly missed that occasion through injury but he shared the frustration of his colleagues who had gone within an ace of ending the wait for silverware that stretched back to 1994.

Of the thirteen men who tackled Rangers on that day there were six survivors for the next cup final appearance, when the

Hampden ghosts were laid to rest. Prince Buaben, Craig Conway, Morgaro Gomis, Gary Kenneth, Mihael Kovacevic and David Robertson all returned for a second bite at the cherry and came away with their appetite for success fulfilled.

The defeat had been painful, but in the long term it demonstrated how close to the Old Firm the new-look Terrors were moving. Levein was determined, ambitious and single-minded. He was intelligent, forward thinking and hard working. It followed that he became hot property and few could grudge him the chance to lead the country he had served with distinction as a player.

Levein had turned around the fortunes not with a magic wand but with a common-sense approach and clarity of thinking that ensured everything suddenly became clear to the Tannadice squad as well as the supporters. After years of muddling through, hoping for harmony, everyone was singing from the same hymn sheet. Sweet music was echoing around Tannadice once again and it was left to Houston to play the role of conductor when Levein moved to the Scotland job in 2009. Houston shares Levein's vision for the club, which has started from the grassroots up, with a revolutionary take on youth coaching and development, and his passion for progress rubs off on his players.

Stephen Simpson said: 'Craig Levein was the man who changed us from a team that had flirted with relegation to one that supporters are confident will be challenging in the top half of the table. There was a bit of uncertainty in the aftermath of Peter Houston's appointment but hopefully he will be able to build on the cup success.'

Individuals, as well as the team, will be looking to progress after the success of 2010. David Goodwillie and Craig Conway grabbed the headlines with their cup final opener, and while Goodwillie took home the SPL Young Player of the Year Award, the work of Daly alongside him in attack did not go unnoticed by the appreciative United fans. The duo finished deadlocked on thirteen goals each at the top of the Tannadice scoring chart at the end of the trophy-winning campaign and it had all the hallmarks of a partnership built to thrive.

The way he has embraced his cult status shows the lighter side to Daly's nature – but he takes his career seriously. Rather than heading off for a hedonistic summer of celebration on the back of the cup success in 2010, he teamed up with team-mate Craig Conway for a pre-pre-season fitness programme to ensure he hit the ground running when Peter Houston's squad gathered at St Andrews for their first session of the new campaign. The 2010/11 season kicked off with Daly as the leader in the pack, having been appointed captain in the wake of the return of Andy Webster to Rangers and the retirement of previous skipper Lee Wilkie.

It was a major departure to hand the armband to a forward rather than the more traditional defensive player. Houston's justification was the respect Daly commanded both within the Tannadice dressing room and among the supporters. The manager also pointed towards his new captain's willingness to speak his mind as another key reason in the decision-making process, hailing the man from the Emerald Isle as the 'outstanding' candidate for the top job on the playing staff. There were few arguments from the supporters who have lifted their man to hero status.

BIBLIOGRAPHY

Dundee United – The Official Centenary History, by Peter Rundo and Mike Watson, Birlinn (2009).

The Jimmy Hill Story, by Jimmy Hill, Hodder and Stoughton (1998).

Pittodrie Idols, by Paul Smith, Black & White Publishing (2009).

A Scottish Soccer Internationalist's Who's Who, Douglas Lamming, Hutton Press (1987).

The Tannadice Encylopedia – A-Z of Dundee United, by Mike Watson, Mainstream (1997).

What's It All About, Ralphie?, by Ralph Milne and Gary Robertson, Black & White Publishing (2009).

Additional archive sources:

The Courier, Dundee
Daily Record, Glasgow
Evening Telegraph, Dundee
The Press and Journal, Aberdeen
The Scotsman, Edinburgh
The Sunday Post, Dundee
scottishfa.co.uk
dundeeunitedfc.co.uk
socawarriors.net
dundeecity.gov.uk